Exotic fly-fishing
IN THE
South Seas

Rising rainbow trout

Exotic fly-fishing
IN THE
South Seas

CHRIS HOLE

Kangaroo Press

To those fly-fishermen who travel in pursuit of happiness

By the same Author: *Heaven on a Stick*

Designed by Wing Ping Tong

© Chris Hole 1996

First published in 1996 by Kangaroo Press Pty Ltd
3 Whitehall Road Kenthurst NSW 2156 Australia
PO Box 6125 Dural Delivery Centre NSW 2158 Australia
Printed in Hong Kong through Colorcraft Ltd

ISBN 0 86417 780 1

CONTENTS

Acknowledgments	6
Preface	7
1 The Maniototo of New Zealand's South Island	9
2 Northeast Victoria	19
3 Lizard Island	27
4 Seven Spirit Bay	36
5 Extraordinary El Questro	45
6 The Remote Cocos (Keeling) Islands	55
7 The Gulf of Carpentaria	63
8 Saltwater Fly-fishing for Big Game	72
9 The Island of Efaté, Vanuatu	78
10 Off Madang in Papua New Guinea	87
Index	95

ACKNOWLEDGMENTS

A FLY-FISHING 'Where to' publication cannot be attempted without the co-operation, sponsorship and advice of the service providers and the companionship of fellow travelling-anglers. It simply can't happen without help. I acknowledge this and thank sincerely a number of kind people and organisations.

In New Zealand: Brian and Christine Thomson and Phil and Marg Waldron, and my fishing companions John Clayton from Australia, Don Haines from America and Jimmy Colenso, a local. In Victoria: Gary and Susan Scholz, Graeme Gibb and Ross Bromley, and Nick Wolstenholme who joined us from England. At Lizard Island: Robyn Pontynen (then manager) and her staff, and Brad and Sarah in *Gamefisher*. At Seven Spirit Bay: Stephen Mitchell (then company manager), the staff at the Lodge, and Bret Swain and Mick Reddy. At El Questro: the flamboyant owners, Will and Celia Burrell, and Jason Hamilton and Buddy Tyson. At Cocos Island: Bob Percy, Pat Abernathy and Signa Knight. In the Gulf of Carpentaria: Greg and Jennifer Bethune, and my fishing companions Vance and Patrick Porter from America, and Mitchell Phillips from Sydney. On the Island of Efaté: Marcus and Vicki Thomson and their family and friends. In Papua New Guinea: Dean Butler, Brett and Vicky Middleton, John and Anna Middleton, and Peter Pakula who fished with me in *Talio*.

In other matters: E.J. Todd and the Alpine Angler helped with tackle and Chris Beech with flies; Arttec Warehouse provided art materials, and Aree Hardy of Ansett International managed my travel program very effectively.

In the end it is the production team who deserve the lion's share of the author's thanks. My particular thanks to Berrick Krahnen of PCtech for his computer advice and to Jo West for her editing. Most of all, my thanks go to Gini, my wife, for the hundreds of hours she spent typing and correcting my material—hours without which this book could not have been completed.

PREFACE

APPARENTLY, in the fishing world at least, 'How to' and 'Where to' books are measurably more popular than anecdotal stories. Maybe that is because anglers don't believe other anglers' stories on account of their own exaggerations; more likely it is born of a need to learn from texts in which there is no room for fabrication. Books are expensive too.

This is a 'Where to' book (with the occasional whiff of 'How to'). It is to be the first of two books following this philosophy for which the travel and research was undertaken in 1995. The second, about Russia and eastern Europe, is being keyed into the computer as the first goes to print. But the trouble with location books is that the reader requires the contents to tell him a lot more than just where to go for a particular type of fishing and how to get there. He is vitally interested in, for example, pre-travel medical and visa requirements, costs and currency, tackle and the best fishing spots, climate and associated clothing, and contacts, addresses and telecommunication numbers. Additionally, he would like to know about accommodation and living conditions, local language, time zones, electrical supplies and other matters. And that is where the trouble starts; information current in 1996 has every reason to change in

Chris Hole at work afloat (GREG BETHUNE)

subsequent years, particularly costs, exchange rates, airline schedules, packages and addresses.

The information given in this book is current at release in 1996, with the following provisos which should be checked by the travelling fly-fisherman as he plans his travels:

- The requirements for visas and medical precautions may be subject to change.
- All prices are given in $US, the most negotiable currency throughout the world. Exchange rates used are US 75 cents to the $AUS, US 65 cents to the $NZ, US .009 cents to the Vanuatu Vatu and US 79 cents to the PNG Kina; these may vary.
- Airline and package costs may vary in time and providers cannot be held to the prices quoted; they are given for guidance and relativity only.
- Package content may be altered by the providers.
- Addresses, phone and fax numbers are subject to alteration. In particular, all Australian phone and fax numbers will change by the end of the millennium to accommodate only four area codes throughout the country. The numbers given in the 'Check-off Lists' are notated with new numbers and the dates of changeover where applicable.

Queries should be directed to TELSTRA INT.61.1800.888.888.

There is also the dilemma of choosing between metric and imperial measurements. I have chosen those most commonly used by the travelling anglers I have met who talk imperial language in matters of tackle and fish, often changing to metric when discussing distances. It is not a perfect world and, until that unwelcome day when we are all uncolourfully common, I will measure things in a language which I think adds to the excitement—doesn't a 220-pound marlin sound much better than a 100-kilos of the same?

Finally it is my fervent hope that other travelling fly-fishermen who read this book will have a go at one or more of the locations I have described. I can guarantee they will not be disappointed.

C. M. G. H.
Canberra, January 1996

1
THE MANIOTOTO OF NEW ZEALAND'S SOUTH ISLAND

DURING the second half of the nineteenth century, goldminers struggled across the wild and unforgiving Maniototo landscape in their quest to reach the rich goldfields around Kyeburn, Naseby, St Bathans and other nearby mountain areas. Flanked to the east by the Rock and Pillar Range, to the west by the North Rough Ridge and the Raggedy Range, to the north by the Hawkdun, Ida and Kakanui mountain ranges, and to the south by the Lammerlaws and Lammermores, the Maniototo region with its abundance of rivers, lakes, burns, dams and its irrigation and hydroelectric systems is never static. From harsh, freezing winters, through river flood and howling north-west gales, to occasional summer tranquillity and autumn colours, its rivers vary as much with irrigation-pumping and hydroelectricity-making as they do with the weather. This is a country to test the very best fly-fisherman. It is not easy and only years of experience can indicate to the angler where to go next under often extreme and changing weather conditions. Yet the rewards are great, and much more satisfying than taking regular-rising fish with relative ease in summer stillness.

In this chapter I will not attempt to give all the answers to this area. Rather, I shall concentrate on a recent visit in November 1994—my seventh—highlighting areas I fished in weather ranging from heavy overnight snow, through howling north-westerlies, to glimpses of spring calm when caddis hatched and the big browns took the Royal Wulff. I'll elaborate geographically with one of my watercolour mudmaps of the area, and informatively with another painting of the most-used flies. I'll even give travel, accommodation and fishing regulation details for the mobile angler, but I won't reveal the deep secrets. These must be learned and kept, as I have learned and kept them, by practice and experience (all part of the enjoyment), and by talking to the locals and fishing with them. When all is said and done, the secrets are theirs. They are a kind and hospitable people living in their harsh, rural, angling playground with its history of

NEW ZEALAND's MANIOTOTO
- A Check-off List for the Travelling Fly-fisherman

PRE-TRAVEL

Visas are required for all but some 36 countries, where exemptions are given for differing durations under special circumstances. New Zealand diplomatic or consular offices should be contacted for details.

CURRENCY

The $NZ is worth approximately US65 cents, depending on currency fluctuations. It is advisable to pre-purchase and use $NZ travellers' cheques in New Zealand to avoid additional in-country exchange costs. In most major towns credit cards are readily accepted.

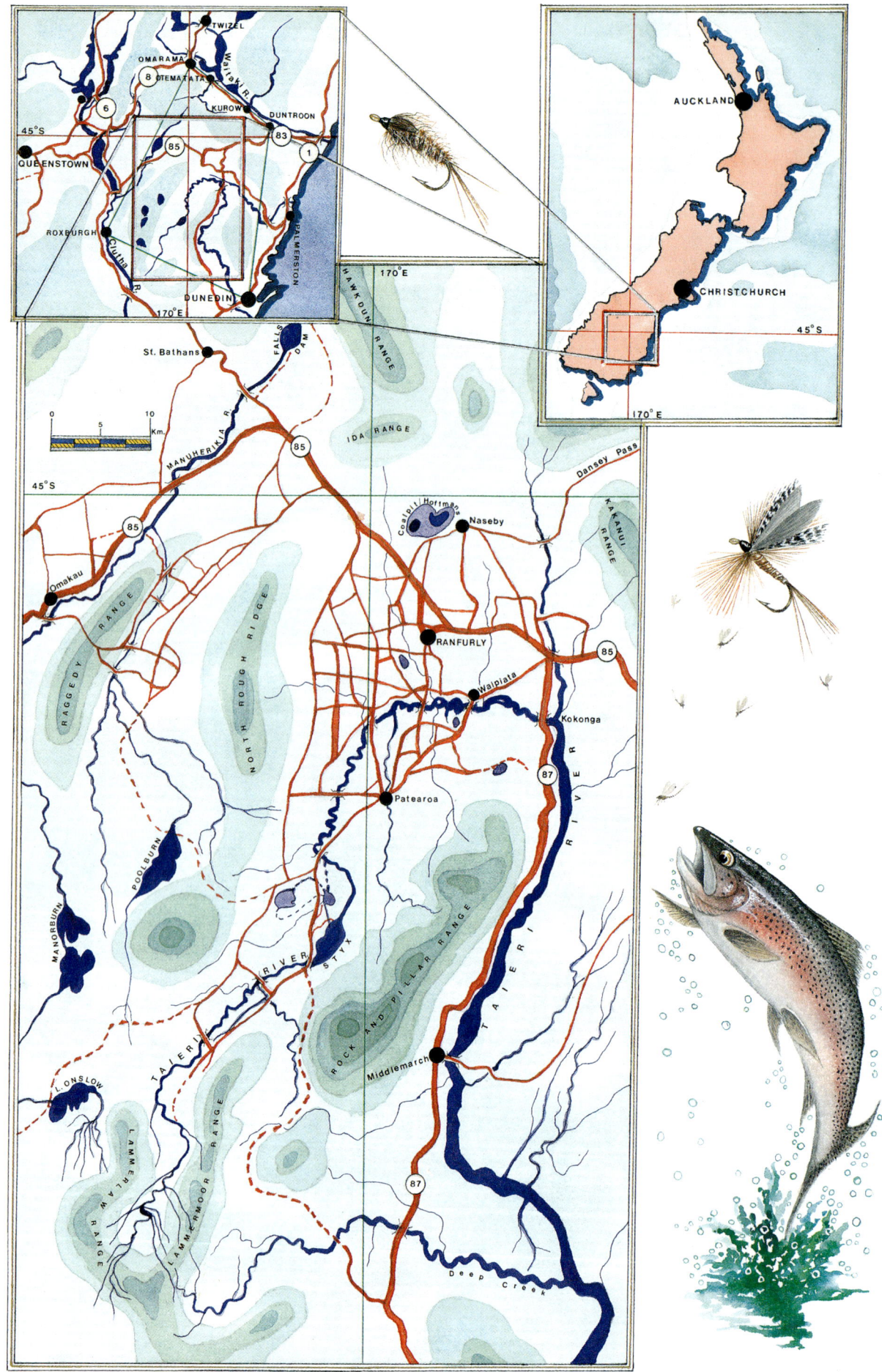

Mudmap of the Maniototo in New Zealand

goldmining traditions. Pragmatically, they foresee increasing fishing pressure as inevitable; wisely, they are doing all they can to promote conservation. Very few of them keep any river fish these days— most are gently returned. Many use barbless hooks by choice, and you can bet your last surviving dollar you will get no local advice unless, as a visitor, you show quite clearly you are willing to do likewise, regardless of regulations in force at the time or whether you have stood the entire Patearoa pub a round of drinks. Conservation is the name of the game in Maniototo.

They are my kind of anglers: good fishermen, good farmers, people whose wry sense of humour has endeared them to me over many years. I can recall once on that last visit when, as dawn broke over Poolburn Reservoir and snow cascaded off the roof of the hut, a bronchial croak was heard from a sleeping bag within: 'Has anyone got any plaster of Paris?'

From a second bag: 'Whadaya want plaster of bloody Paris for?'

First bag: 'I have this giant erection and I want to make a cast of it to take home to Helga...otherwise she'll never believe me.'

Howls of laughter from bags two to five and another day chasing Maniototo browns has begun.

On another occasion, this time on the banks of a river north of the Maniototo, some of the occupants of the sleeping-bags were examining an extensive backwater from a steep cliff. Below them big browns were cruising, and the anglers decided to return at dusk to river level on the river side of the backwater arm where there might be a vague chance of hooking a monster in the diminishing light. But on return at sunset a crazy old gaffer is seen on the cliff top, bombing the trout below with rocks, trying to get them to move into the fast water at the river's edge where, with pre-positioned tackle, he hopes to snare them. The occupants of the sleeping-bags debate whether to push the silly old fool off the cliff, but decide that two

The 'Plaster of Paris' hut

wrongs (and a likely manslaughter charge) don't equal one right, and they go upstream instead to fish with extraordinary success in a caddis hatch of plague proportions.

And a final story, if I may? When the weather, not unusually for the Maniototo, was simply appalling, the sleeping-bag occupants stopped fishing and retired to the Ranfurly Motel one night, complete with a gallon jar of Johnnie Walker and half a dozen eggs (the fishermen were never really strong on dietary needs). And, after helping to empty the jar, one of the occupants announces he will demonstrate the amazing and devilishly clever 'Mexican raw-egg Trick'. He places a glass of water near the edge of the kitchenette table and covers it with a flat sheet of cardboard so that its edge stands proud of the table top. Then, centrally on the cardboard, he stands a tube of stiff paper and balances a raw egg on top so that it is immediately above the glass. Next, taking the kitchenette whisk-broom, he places the straw end under the table and holds it in place with his foot while pulling the handle end back under the pressure of the bent straw. Having thus set the scene, he asks the other characters to sit opposite and announces: 'When I let this broom handle go it will knock the cardboard and the tube away, and the egg will fall harmlessly into that glass of water!'

As they subsequently help to clean up the kitchenette—and themselves—the other bag occupants express their deep gratitude that there were only six eggs in the box, and suggest that the magician should procure another jar of whisky. . .'as it's going to be a long night'.

Never was the adage that 'fishing is more than just catching fish' truer than on the Maniototo.

Travelling to the Maniototo

Together with my old fishing friend, John Clayton, I flew from Sydney to Christchurch on the regular Qantas/Air New Zealand service at 9 am on Wednesday, 9 November 1994. From Christchurch we took a regular internal flight to Dunedin to stay overnight with friends before driving to Patearoa in the Maniototo the next day. Dunedin is probably a little closer to the Maniototo than Queenstown, which is the other option when trying to reach the area from Christchurch, and it is possible to go all the way in one day by collecting a rental car at either destination, both of which are the last outposts for rentals before the Maniototo. Travellers can also go by bus from Christchurch to Palmerston, Queenstown or Dunedin but there are no further bus connections to the Maniototo. There are no car rentals at Palmerston, and bus travel entails an overnight stop in Christchurch.

For overseas travellers not connecting through Sydney, most international carriers fly daily in and out of Auckland in the North Island, from where same-day connections can be made to Christchurch and all points south using internal airlines. Once in the Maniototo, however, a car is essential but not necessarily a four-wheel drive. Also, some good guiding services will collect anglers at Christchurch

TRAVEL

There are daily return flights from Sydney to Christchurch, with same day connections to Dunedin and Queenstown. The return economy fare is approximately $US550. For incoming international anglers travelling through the North Island, there are daily flights in and out of Auckland. There are also daily connections to the south where a return economy flight—Auckland to Dunedin, for example—is approximately $US300 (if included as a package). As we go to print a new, Kiwi Air, once-weekly service from Sydney to Dunedin and return on Fridays has started at a cost of $US340 return.

CAR RENTALS

These are available from Dunedin and Queenstown from approximately $US50 per day for a small compact car with unlimited mileage and insurance (but to waive the $US450 insurance excess the cost rises by $US4.50 per day). Gasoline costs are around US 65 cents per litre.

airport as part of their package, but these services are normally based some distance from the Maniototo: for example, at Omarama and Twizel further north in the Waitaki Valley.

Accommodation

Comfortable accommodation can be found in the Maniototo at very reasonable prices at the Ranfurly Lion Hotel and the Ranfurly Motel in Ranfurly, where there is also a good camping ground with caravan and tent sites and all modern facilities. Anglers can also stay at the Patearoa Hotel cabins. Further north there is good accommodation at Naseby and in the Dansey Pass Hotel (infamous for honeymooners and 'illicit' weekenders) but both of these places are some distance from most Maniototo fishing, which is an important factor when considering dawn and dusk rises. On the other hand they are closer to the Waitaki system where there is also superb fly-fishing. . .in which case it would be more expedient to stay at Kurow or Otematata where there are more hotels, motels and camping grounds.

Guiding

To the best of my knowledge there are no dedicated guides operating in the Maniototo, although there was one at Ranfurly in the 1980s. I always stay with my friends and, by virtue of years of experience and because I actively pursue conservation measures, I have been privileged to learn some of their secrets. It behoves the visitor to act similarly when the locals may offer some assistance. But, even for the uninitiated, there is an awful lot of water in the Maniototo—and it's all good.

On the north side of the Ida Range, out of the Maniototo and into the Waitaki Valley, there are a number of good guides based at Omarama and Twizel. These guides can guarantee good fish for the angler from the streams and tributaries flowing into the Waitaki system and from the lake system itself. No doubt, also, they will soon be exploring further south into the Taieri Plain.

The Waters

The predominant river of the Maniototo is the Taieri. This multi-meandering, tea-coloured, brown trout haven, which rises in the Lammerlaw Range and runs northwards under three bridges before being dammed in the Styx Gorge, is one of the great trout rivers of this world. It also provides power for two stations downstream from the Styx, and caters for the multi-million dollar Maniototo irrigation scheme through very fishable canals and dams. (It is of interest that the locals paid for the completion of this scheme when government finance dried up.) From Hores Bridge, after the Styx Gorge, the Taieri wobbles its way north again, then east under four more bridges before passing south of Ranfurly and disappearing under Kokonga Bridge (which carries the road to Middlemarch and Dunedin), and turning southwards when it seems to become no longer so attractive to trout.

ACCOMMODATION

RANFURLY LION HOTEL
Charlemont Street (SH85) Ranfurly
Phone/Fax: INT.(0)3.444.9140
From $US25 per person/day

RANFURLY MOTEL
Davis Avenue Ranfurly
Phone: INT.(0)3.444.9383
From $US20 per person/day

RANFURLY CAMPING GROUND
Reade Street Ranfurly
Phone: INT.(0)3.444.9144
From $US15 per site/day

NASEBY CAMPING GROUND
Phone: INT.(0)3.444.9904
From $US15 per site/day

PATEAROA HOTEL UNITS
Patearoa
Phone: INT.0(3).444.7865
From $US15 per person/day

DANSEY PASS HOTEL
Dansey Pass
Phone/Fax: INT.0(3).444.9048
From $US35 per person/day.

IN-TOWN FACILITIES

Ranfurly has a reasonable range of restaurants, shops, banks, garages, and health services (including a hospital).

TIME ZONE

All of New Zealand is 12 hours ahead of Greenwich Mean Time, with an additional hour added for Summer Time from October through March.

ELECTRICITY

New Zealand operates on 240 volt AC supply.

CLIMATE AND CLOTHING

The weather can change abruptly at almost any time of the year. During the prime fishing season from November through April, anglers should be prepared to fish in warm, balmy days altering to snowfalls and predominant north-west winds. The area is mainly dry and a hat and sunscreen are essential.

Fishing the Waitaki

A seven-pound rainbow in a Waitaki feeder stream

The other great river in the Maniototo (or nearby, anyway) is the Manuherikia, a glacial trout stream that rises in the Hawkdun Range and runs south through Falls Dam, then west of the Raggedy Range to join the mighty Clutha south of Alexandra.

But that is not all. The impounded waters of the Maniototo, whether hydroelectric, irrigation, rural or recreational, are very extensive. They range from big impoundments like Lake Onslow, and Manorburn, Greenland and Poolburn reservoirs in the west, to smaller farm dams such as Hamiltons, Blakeleys and Johnsons, to recreational waters like the Coalpit and Hoffmans. These still waters with their individuality allow for angling almost regardless of abrupt changes in the weather, as long as the right place is chosen (and that can only be determined by experience).

Regulations

All trout fishing in New Zealand is licensed. Costs vary depending

Maniototo Trout Flies

on duration, from full season to weekly and three-day licences, to one-day. With each licence comes a colour-coded chart of the local waters, detailing where and when, minimum sizes, permitted baits and lures, bag limits, whether boating is allowed, exceptions and extensions. Further details, such as fish-tagging programs and how the angler can help management, are issued from time to time. It is a well-managed system which is easily understood and helps greatly in the preservation of some of the very best trout fishing in the world.

The opening and closing of the season varies a little from area to area and river to river. Explicit details come with the fishing licence, but it would be reasonable to say that the best part of the season is from November through March.

Flies

The 'hot' flies at night in the Maniototo are the Black Gnat and Twilight Beauty (sizes 12 to 14) with small Black Muddlers coming a close second. During the early morning the Kakahi Queen and Hare and Copper Nymph (both about size 14) are good, but throughout daylight the Royal Wulff (12 to 16) comes into a class of its own representing, it would seem, either the hatched caddis or the damselfly.

November 1994

The majority of the 1994 visit—certainly the first two of the three weeks—was spent looking for shelter, examining backwaters and dams, and seeking insect hatches in very poor weather: conditions in which one is forced to work very hard at one's fishing, and when techniques often improve accordingly. The rivers were high and discoloured with fish seldom feeding after 7 am and before 8 pm, so the backwaters, lakes, dams and canals were fished during the day.

My first fish was a brown of four and a half pounds taken on the Hare and Copper Nymph from the Taieri at 7 am on the first day. Some miles upstream from where this first fish was taken, a tiny glacial burn, surrounded by willows, joins the main river. Upstream in the burn the water flows from a shallow willow-edged water race into a short rocky gorge which can be crossed by a wooden bridge. Below the bridge the water widens into a deep green pool before spilling out over pebbles on its way to join the main river. Hidden under the rocks below the bridge, but darting out into the main current to feed from time to time, was a brown of considerable proportions—not a long fish, but a very fat one. Throughout that three-week visit we took daily turns trying to entice him to the fly, but whenever we started to spot and call the shots for casting, he would somehow sense a presence in his 'rear-vision mirror' and dive for cover under a rocky overhang. Size estimates varied from six to eight pounds, but no matter what tactics were used (and some were wondrous indeed) we never got near him. He remains for someone else. . .if the locals will tell where he is.

In the poor weather we found there was some respite in the mornings from about 5 until 7 before the wind started to blow. This was particularly so along the weedy edges of the lakes and dams where the

GUIDING

Guides can be contracted from Omarama and Twizel to the north and some will collect anglers from Christchurch airport. Additionally, most charge an all-up rate for transport, meals, accommodation and guiding ranging around $US200 per day. Not many, however, are known to operate south into the Maniototo—although they may in time. One new guide with an increasing reputation is:
Will Spry
P.O. Box 7, Twizel. New Zealand
Phone/Fax: INT.64.(0)3.4350135.

LICENCES

These can be obtained through guides, tackle stores, outfitters and many other outlets and general stores throughout the Maniototo. Costs are approximately:
Season: $US36
Weekly: $US15
Three-day: $US11
One-day: $US7

The best part of the season is from November through March.

TACKLE

Most fly-fishing is done using eight- to nine-foot, five- to six-weight outfits and matched floating lines with about 100 yards of backing. The best flies include: Royal Wulff (14–16), Black Gnat and Twilight Beauty (12–14), Black Muddler (12), Kakahi Queen (12–16), and Hare and Copper Nymph (12–18). Six-pound tippets are normally used, but may have to be fined to five- and even four-pound in very clear conditions.

fish would chase nymphs and small smelt for a hearty breakfast before retiring deep until evening. And in the evening the activity would start just after sunset and continue for two hours with most of the action taking place on top, the trout often gorging themselves on both emerging caddis and the fully emerged insect as well, all dark-coloured.

At one point during the visit, John and I returned to Dunedin to collect a car. Taking the route through Palmerston meant crossing the Shag River about an hour out of Ranfurly. Despite the foul weather, no fisherman crosses a bridge without stopping to look. And there they were! Maybe ten browns up to five pounds, taking caddis regularly from the surface. But, my heaven, they were spooky. There was no way down from the bridge without being seen, then one was faced with almost impenetrable willows on both banks. So there were no hook-ups. But it is worth a carefully planned visit in the future; although not strictly in the Maniototo, the Shag is a very exciting river.

Towards the end of the visit we left the Maniototo and drove to Hawea where we had some success with rainbows in the Hawea River, and on to Wanaka to stay with Don and Gayle Haines from America. Don had looked after me admirably when I fished Idaho, Montana and Wyoming in 1992. From Wanaka we drove north and east through the Lindis Pass, into the Waitaki Valley to meet more old friends and to fish again in those superb rivers (and their tributaries) that run into the Waitaki. On the first day I hooked 28 fish, landing and releasing 12, with the biggest topping five pounds. On the second the results were similar with my biggest being a six and a half pounder taken on a Royal Wulff, a beautiful fish which rose slowly from 20 feet down to gulp the fly in classic fashion.

The Waitaki Valley is also easily reached from the Maniototo via the Dansey Pass and we returned that way. As previously mentioned, local guides are available at Omarama and Twizel, although not all have access through some of the locked gates on privately owned property in the area. Locked gates notwithstanding, this whole part of New Zealand's South Island, roughly contained by a line joining Omarama to Duntroon, to Dunedin, to Roxburgh and back to Omarama again, is one of the my most favourite fly-fishing locations.

My good fly-fishing friend from the Maniototo, Brian Thomson, runs the general store at Patearoa with his wife Christine. Brian may offer some good advice to the visitor if approached carefully, but probably only to the fly-fisherman who puts conservation above all else. On the other hand Christine was happy to part with the recipes which follow. We would always take a jar of her choc chippie biscuits on our fishing forays and it would inevitably be returned empty. As for the trout recipe, Christine believes (as I and many others do) that trout should be cooked simply if they are to retain their delicate flavour. Moreover, we only eat Maniototo trout very occasionally and then only trout from impounded waters—all river fish are released.

Choc Chippie Biscuits

125 g butter
150 g sugar
1½ tbsp condensed milk
1 tsp vanilla essence
1 tsp baking powder
175 g flour
50 g dark chocolate chips

MIX the butter and sugar, add the condensed milk, vanilla essence, and the flour combined with the baking powder and chocolate chips.
ROLL the mixture into small balls, place on a baking tray and flatten with a fork. Bake at 150°C until light brown (15–20 minutes).

Trout Steaks

1 five-pound trout, filleted, boned and
  cut into steaks (three to a fillet)
2 eggs
Breadcrumbs
Lemon pepper
Salt and black pepper

BEAT the eggs with salt and black pepper in a bowl. In a separate bowl mix the breadcrumbs and lemon pepper. Wash the trout steaks in the egg mixture and then in the breadcrumbs, ensuring a good coating.
PAN-FRY in oil or butter until golden brown. Serve with slices of lemon or lime, and tartare sauce if desired.

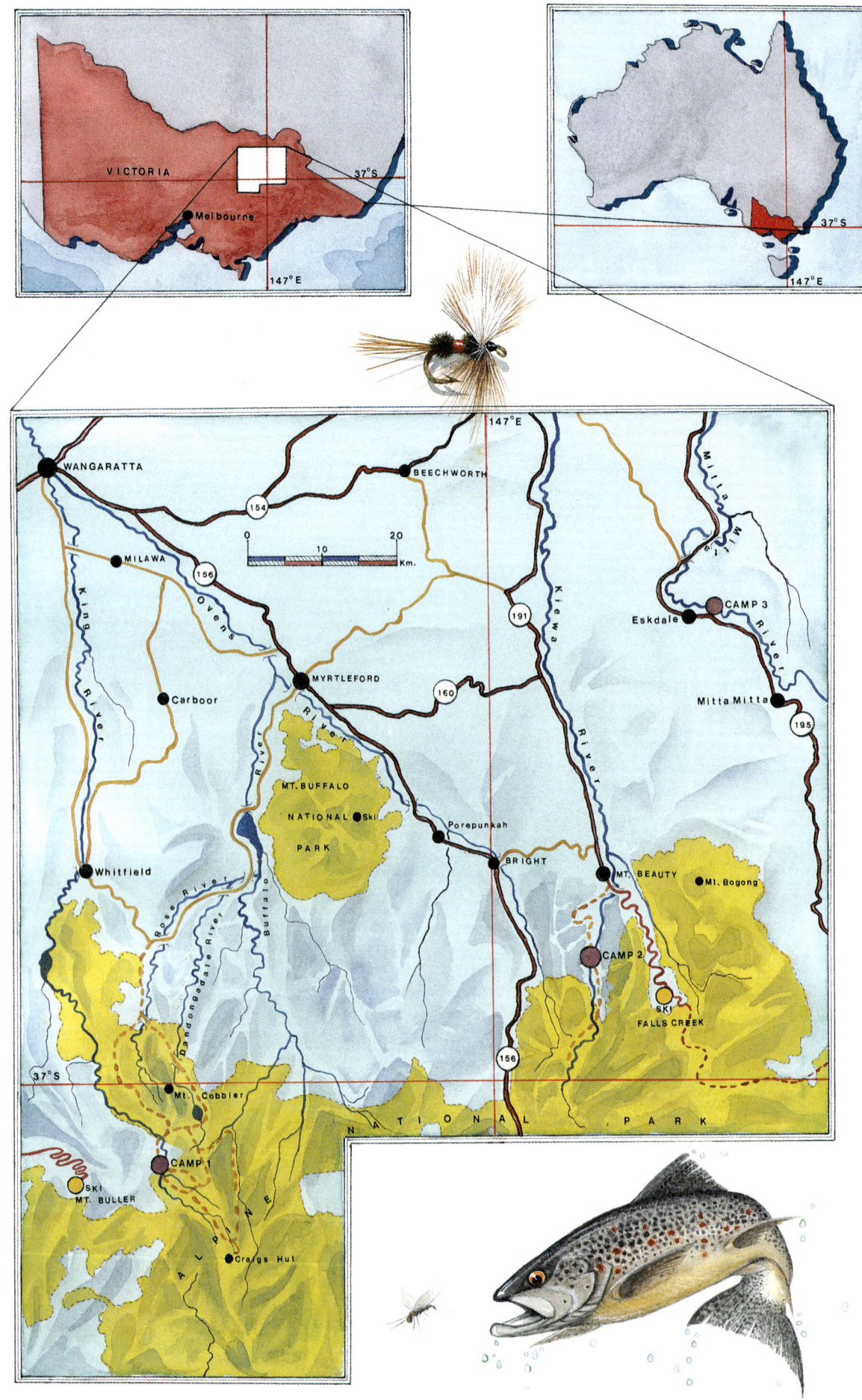

Mudmap of the northeast Victorian trout region

2
NORTHEAST VICTORIA

A HEAVY MIST blanketed the Mitta Mitta River on the first autumn morning I ever fished there in the mid 1980s when there were redfin as well as trout in the rapids. But it didn't stop me drifting a Black Nymph beside a willow-covered bank to hook a four-pound rainbow.

Ten years later, having clambered and fished over much of the Alpine National Park, I returned to the Mitta in the summer of 1995 with four friends to find many changes in the watery scene. While there were still

LEFT
Victorian alpine country

RIGHT
Resting at Craigs Hut (l to r) Graeme, Gary and Nick

good trout for the taking, the river was supporting an increasing population of the dreaded European carp, the water was less clear than I remembered, indeed my memory bubble seemed to collapse. Sometimes one's memories should be allowed to remain forever and not be destroyed by the reality of a revisit. Yet there is something beautiful about that alpine scenery; something that entices one to return, and return again. It is little wonder Craigs Hut on Mount Clear was chosen for the filming of *The Man from Snowy River*. But, as we stood there on a still, summer morning, gazing across the Alps, I said to my companions that I reckoned Kirk Douglas had never clambered in; more probably he clattered in by helicopter for filming each day.

In the high country of that part of the Great Divide mountain chain known as the Australian Alps, human history can be traced back 20,000 years when Aborigines were known to live in caves around the Snowy River valley. About 15,000 years ago, as the valleys grew warmer, they moved to higher country.

In the 1820s, following the opening up of the high country by European explorers Strzelecki, McMillan, Hume and Hovell, McKillop, von Mueller and von Guerard, pastoralists from the country centred around Port Jackson (now Sydney), 'squatted' (that is, took up land without payment to the Government), and cultivated the valleys between the mountains of the Australian Alps. More pastures meant more stock could be fed, and more stock meant more profit. Cattle runs were opened up and slab huts built, some of which have been repaired and remain as monuments to the past and shelters for the present. In the 1850s fortune seekers started an intensive search for gold. In the first half of the twentieth century, a scheme was devised to harness the waters of the Kiewa River for hydroelectricity. Work on this was finished in 1961, but even though the project was overshadowed by the Commonwealth's prestigious Snowy Scheme, the beautiful Rocky Valley Lake remains, a monument to a dream of an earlier industrial age.

The first attempt to introduce salmonids into Victoria was in 1864 using 11 boxes of salmon ova left over from the original *Norfolk/Victoria* shipment to Tasmania, where it all began that year on the River Plenty. The resulting fry were released in Badgers Creek near Healesville, but did not survive. For nearly 20 years, attempts continued to hatch salmonid ova and release fry in Victoria, with initially a number of failures but finally with success. It was not until the early 1880s, however, that trout reached northeastern Victoria, coinciding a little later, in 1887, with the first introduction of trout in the nearby Monaro region of New South Wales, thus providing the beginnings of the sport of trout fishing across the Great Dividing Range of southeastern mainland Australia. It was a flourishing sport until the 1980s when lack of good management, born of political pressure from much increased angler numbers, has marked its unnecessary decline. Increased angler pressures require tighter control to protect the resource, not reduced regulation to appease the voting masses.

NORTHEAST VICTORIA
- A Check-off List for the Travelling Fly-fisherman

PRE-TRAVEL

Some overseas visitors will require visas to visit Australia. Australian diplomatic or consular offices should be contacted for details.

CURRENCY

The $AUS is worth approximately US75 cents depending on currency fluctuations. It is advisable to pre-purchase and use $AUS travellers' cheques in Australia to avoid additional in-country exchange costs. All major credit cards are accepted in the area.

TRAVEL

There are daily flights from Sydney and Melbourne to Albury and the return fare is from $US170 and $US130 respectively. Landcruiser four-wheel drive wagons can be pre-booked for delivery to Albury airport or collected at Benalla. Hire charges are $US75 per day (with 200 free kilometres per day and a $US375 insurance excess). Fuel costs are approximately US60 cents per litre. The contact for car hire is:
Rose City Self-drive, Benalla.
Victoria 3620
Phone: INT.61.(0)57.623382 (From November 1996: 61.(0)3.57623382)
Fax: INT.61.(0)57.623022 (From November 1996: 61.(0)3.57623022)

Travel to Northeast Victoria

The nearest major airport serving the Victorian Alpine National Park area is at the large inland town of Albury, some 72 kilometres northeast of Wangaratta on the Hume Highway (31) joining Sydney and Melbourne. There are daily domestic flights to and from Albury from both Sydney and Melbourne, and less frequent flights connecting other major cities, some of which require a flight change. Once in the area a four-wheel drive vehicle is necessary to visit the upper reaches of the most productive rivers. These vehicles can be pre-booked from nearby Benalla to be available on arrival at Albury airport.

Alternatively, those travelling locally in their own vehicles, should plan to head generally in the direction of Albury/Wangaratta and turn southeast towards Myrtleford, Bright, Mount Beauty or Mitta Mitta.

Accommodation and Guiding

Good hotel and motel accommodation is available throughout the area at reasonable prices, but to be close to the good fishing one would need to choose Myrtleford, Bright, Mount Beauty, Eskdale or Mitta. As some of the tracks into the river-source fishing are rough, once in the area, most fishermen find it more convenient to set up camp. With the surrounding mountains and the stream at one's feet, this can be very exhilarating and extremely enjoyable.

For visitors new to the area, I would recommend a night or so at the Hermitage Motor Inn at Wangaratta. This motel is central and very comfortable but, importantly, the owner, Ross Bromley, is a very keen fisherman, a capable guide and a member of the Wangaratta Fly-fishing Club. Time spent with Ross being briefed on local geography, the rivers and the conditions can mean the difference between a successful and a mediocre visit.

The only other guides I know who operate in the area are Mike Spry of Spry Fly who occasionally drifts as far west as the Mitta from his base at Khancoban in New South Wales, and for those starting from Melbourne, Mark Weigall's 'The Trout School' is very capable at handling northeast Victorian requirements.

The Waters

The best of the King River fishing (in the southwest of the area) is to be found upstream from Whitfield, and this requires a four-wheel drive for access. It includes some of the most ruggedly beautiful scenery in Australia, with gorges dropping hundreds of feet to bubbling, gurgling trout water. On my visit I found browns and rainbows in roughly equal proportions, and in summer they feed steadily from seemingly endless hatches of caddis, duns and spinners. It is a hard slog to reach the best spots and the fish are not that big when you get there, but it is worth it for the scenery alone. I would, however, strongly recommend obtaining detailed geographic advice (from Ross for example) before venturing into this part of the Alpine National Park, as it is an area of many confusing sidetracks. Once inside, access to the Rose, Dandongadale

ACCOMMODATION

HERMITAGE MOTOR INN
Cnr Cusack and Mackay Streets,
Wangaratta. Victoria 3677
Phone: INT.61.(0)57.217444 (From November 1996: 61.(0)3.57217444
Fax: INT.61.(0)57.221812 (From November 1996: 61.(0)3.57221812)
(Proprietor: Ross Bromley who can also advise on fishing).

FACILITIES

All major towns in the area contain restaurants, shops, motels, hotels, banks, garages and health services.

TIME ZONE

The time zone in Eastern Australia is ten hours ahead of Greenwich Mean Time with an additional hour added for Summer Time between October and March.

ELECTRICITY

Australia operates on 240 volt AC supply.

CLIMATE AND CLOTHING

During the height of the fishing season from November through March, the days are normally warm to hot with cool to cold nights. However, rain jackets should be included and a hat, sunscreen and insect repellent are essential.

and Buffalo Rivers is also possible and can be rewarding, and a visit to Craigs Hut a very worthwhile diversion.

On this recent visit we did not fish the Ovens River. Rather, we travelled to Mount Beauty and south on rough tracks to the west branch of the Kiewa River, only five kilometres direct from the source of the Ovens, but far removed over a mountain ridge. The top of the Kiewa is in very steep country requiring a slog similar to the King but which was, for us, more rewarding, with a bag of 30-plus browns and rainbows being taken and released on our best day. It is a river which can be waded upstream with little difficulty; the hard part is getting down into the river at the beginning of the day, and the even harder part is getting up and out at day's end.

A King River dun

I briefly described my recent disappointment with the Mitta Mitta River at the start of this chapter. It is a river of easy access running along a valley floor with undulating hills either side. It is dammed not far from its source at Dartmouth and runs north until it enters Lake Hume near Albury to join the Murray system. Despite the carp and the associated water discolouration, it still shows some beautifully clear runs and glides and is home to trout in excess of four pounds, although the average would be nearer to one. It is also renowned for its spectacular evening rise in summer when the angler can experience an hour of frenetic fun casting a large, bushy Royal Wulff. In daytime its trout are very selective and spooky.

The Regulations

Although Amateur Fishing Licences (of one month, one year, or three years duration) are mandatory in Victoria, specific regulations to protect and conserve wild salmonid stocks are practically non-existent. There is no closed season to protect spawning fish; there are no bag limits; size limits only apply in a few stated impoundments; bait restrictions and taking-methods are a farce, and it would appear, once again, that the authorities have little interest in the protection of wild salmonids for the future. Fly-fishing clubs and recreational fishing authorities are doing what they can to redress this unfortunate situation but it is a slow process.

The Tackle and the Flies

Because of the confined fishing in these alpine waters, three- to five-weight fly rods of no more than eight feet in length are probably the best. As for flies: when I asked my Victorian friends what they considered to be the most successful half dozen for the area, they waited until I returned from fishing one evening and presented me with a rough-whittled piece of pine on which were mounted six flies, from size 8 (longshank) to size 16—all Royal Wulffs! I must agree that the Wulff was undeniably the most consistently successful fly, but we also achieved good things with the Brown Nymph, the Elk-hair Caddis, the Red Ant, and that New Zealand fly which seems to keep hooking trout the world over, the Kakahi Queen.

Trout flies of northeast Victoria

The February 1995 Visit

Nick Wolstenholme, the son of a retired Royal Navy friend who was helping me to plan a fly-fishing foray to Russia later in 1995, arrived in Australia on one of those post-school, pre-university visits in time to travel to Victoria with me on Thursday 23 February. Nick had fished with me before when his father was stationed in Australia some years earlier. It was a pleasure to include him to repay his father's kindness and because I knew he could handle a fly rod well, and he carried his own tackle wherever he went.

We drove from Canberra to Wangaratta together to spend the night with Gary Scholz and his family before tackling the rivers the following day. Gary is another keen and competent fly-fisherman and, at the time, was President of the Council of Victorian Fly-fishers. I had met him in 1994 and subsequently asked him to advise me about fishing in his area when a previous plan to concentrate on the Mitta for this visit had to be abandoned when that river went into spate when Dartmouth Dam was opened to feed downstream irrigation following the 1994/95 drought. (As it turned out, of course, by the time we reached the Mitta it was back to normal.)

An hour before dawn on Friday 24 February Gary, Nick and I left Gary's house, picked up some ice in Wangaratta and drove to Carboor to collect Graeme Gibb, a farmer, fly-fisherman and mountain trekker whom Gary had arranged to be our guide over the days that followed. From Carboor we drove onwards through Whitfield and the Rose River Valley, and upwards on rough dirt tracks into the Alpine National Park. We skirted Mount Cobbler to the west and dropped down into the King River Valley to set up our first camp at Pineapple Flat. On the way in, Graeme related the story of one of his first visits to the area. Apparently, as a boy, he had been dropped near Pineapple Flat together with a friend, their gear, and a tin dinghy in which they planned to travel down the King, fishing as they went, to a prearranged pick-up point. The trouble was that when they packed their gear into the boat, it sat firmly on the rocks in the river which was unexpectedly very low after drought. Their inbound transport had left them and they had no option other than to cut two saplings, sling the boat and their gear between them and walk out—all 20 kilometres through the mountains!

Later I was made aware that Graeme had retained his fitness and mountaineering ability when, after setting up camp beside the river at 10.30 that morning, the four of us scrambled for two hours through near-vertical scrub downstream to rejoin the river and fish up for the rest of the day. On reaching the water at the end of the trek in, I sat right down in its icy clarity on a rock, regaining some strength in the 35°C heat, just trying to imagine what it would be like trying to carry a dinghy out of those mountains.

But we were soon recovered sufficiently to start fishing the crystal-clear mountain water as it cascaded over rocks and into green pools. Progress upstream was relatively easy—certainly a lot easier than skirting the stream on the cliffs which we did on the way in so that we wouldn't disturb the fish. In any case there were fish to think about and beautiful

GUIDING

Good advice can be obtained from Ross Bromley at the Hermitage Motor Inn in Wangaratta. For dedicated guiding, services are provided by:
  Mike Spry
  P.O. Box 7
  Khancoban
  New South Wales 2642
  Phone: INT.61.(0)60.769511
  (From August 1997: 61.(0)2.60769511)
  Fax: INT.61.(0)60.769496
  (From August 1977: 61.(0)2.60769496)

Or, if coming direct from Melbourne, guiding and tuition can be arranged through:
  Mark Weigall
  The Trout School
  2/87 Earl Street
  Kew
  Victoria 3101
  Phone: INT.61.(0)3.98537884
  Mobile: 61.(0)3.015360458
  Free call: INT.1800.655764

willows, and water and sky to look at (one doesn't see much when bashing through tea tree on a cliff face). We caught and released a number of small fish, mainly rainbows, most of them taking the Royal Wulff or a caddis pattern. Rounding one corner, Gary spooked a big brown and later we were both broken by good fish. Apart from these we reached camp around 7 pm, happily exhausted but with a smallish fish count, both in numbers and size.

On the morning of Saturday 25 February we broke camp at 9 o'clock and left the area taking a scenic but rough route to visit Craigs Hut before leaving the park in the vicinity of the Dandongadale and Rose Rivers. At one point during this trek I turned a hairpin right-hander to be faced with 'the staircase' ahead on a track the width of a Landcruiser, a cliff face on the left, and vertical 500-foot drop on the right. The staircase consisted of granite steps rising about 15 inches at a time; there was no going back; so in low-ratio diff-lock, and with the passengers closing their eyes, up we went. We drove out through Myrtleford in shimmering heat, turned southeast to Mount Beauty and continued on rough dirt tracks again to our second camp on a flat in the gorge of the west branch of the Kiewa River. It had been a hot and hard driving day and that icy river, a cold beer and a camp-fire dinner were very, very welcome.

On 26 February we decided to split the river. I dropped Gary and Graeme some distance downstream to fish up to a pre-planned position where Nick and I left the Landcruiser for them to drive back to camp, and from where we two tumbled down the cliffs to the river to fish upstream to the same, camp rendezvous point. Apart from one bust-off, a couple of small fish, and a splashy escape from a swimming tiger snake, Nick and I achieved little on the upstream section while the others below us did well, accounting for some 25 fish, many of which took Gary's Red Ant.

We broke camp at 8.20 the next morning and retraced our path to Mount Beauty, then turned north on Highway 191 and southeast to join Highway 195 (and the Mitta) near Eskdale. At midday we met Ross Bromley at the local pub and drove down to the river flats to set up our final camp.

Fish were seen rising to a hatch in the early afternoon heat but they were very spooky and soon went deep until sundown. We fished into the afternoon with Nick scoring the only success in fast water, and with carp clearly visible in numbers in the muddy edges of the still pools. In the evening we deployed for the much-awaited evening rise only to be frustrated when a cool windy change came in with scudding showers right on twilight.

A damp night, a quiet morning, and a counter lunch at the Eskdale pub marked the end of the Victorian expedition, which was well worth it if only for the company and the mountain scenery. We dropped Graeme at Carboor on the way back to Wangaratta and spent the night at Gary's house before going our separate ways the next day: Gary back to work, Nick fruit picking to make some money, and me back to Canberra.

LICENCES AND REGULATIONS

Licences can be obtained through guides, tackle stores, outfitters and many other outlets and general stores throughout the area. A copy of the sparse regulations is issued at the same time. Licences can be obtained for:
  28 days: $US7.50
  one year: $US15
  three years: $US45

TACKLE

Most fishing is done with eight-foot, three- to five-weight outfits and matched floating lines with about 75 yards of backing. The best flies include the Royal Wulff (8–14), the Brown Nymph (10–14), the Red Ant (12–14), the Elk-hair Caddis (10–12), and the Kakahi Queen (10–14). Three- to five-pound tippets are normally used.

Rising brown trout

As always with fly-fishermen, we ate and drank well. Gary was our chef at the camp-fire dinners which were washed down with some excellent local reds (Brown Brothers of Milawa are famous for some exceptional wines and well worth a visit when in the area). If, however, I was limited to only one recipe from Gary's camp oven it would be his 'Eggplant in Herbs'.

Gary's Eggplant in Herbs

1 eggplant
2 eggs
½ cup self-raising flour
¼ handful of mixed herbs
Oil

SLICE the eggplant into five ml slices.
BEAT two eggs and dip the eggplant into them.
IN a medium-size plastic bag place the flour and the herbs and mix thoroughly.
SHAKE the dipped eggplant in the flour and herb mixture in the bag.
FRY in oil in a heavy-base camp oven or pan, turning until golden brown on both sides.

3
LIZARD ISLAND

Saltwater flies of Lizard Island

Location descriptions, whether of the good or the bad, roll out as exaggerated clichés. For the good: 'the best in the world' (thousands of the same?), 'without peer' (ditto), 'this is paradise' (I thought life was meant to be militant here on earth)...and so on. Yet Lizard Island probably comes closest to deserving such praise. Lying off the coast of far-north Queensland, 270 kilometres north of Cairns, 93 kilometres northeast of Cooktown and surrounded by the Great Barrier Reef, it is soaked in tropical everything, effortlessly comfortable and luxurious, totally relaxed, and thoroughly deserving of the nickname 'the jewel in the Reef'.

For many thousands of years, Aborigines travelled the 27 kilometres from the mainland by canoe to Lizard Island to collect food from the shores and shallow reefs. The first Europeans to make a recorded visit were Captain James Cook and the ship's company of HMS *Endeavour* when they anchored off the island in August 1770 for a brief respite as they tried to find a way out of the Great Barrier Reef. Cook climbed the 1200-foot peak, now known as Cook's Look, twice, in the hope of sighting an escape route through the surrounding coral, but because of the haze he had to follow his observations by sending a small boat to the outer reefs for further examination. A narrow opening was eventually found, which Cook named Providence Passage, now known as Cook's Passage. He also named the island after the large but harmless monitor lizards (sometimes called sand goannas) that still inhabit it.

In the following years the area was visited and surveyed by HM Ships *Beagle*, *Fly* and *Rattlesnake*, and in 1887, HMS *Albert* anchored off the island and the ship's surgeon observed the proliferation of *bêche-de-mer*, or sea cucumber, which was later harvested commercially by a settler, Robert Watson and his family, using Chinese help. This venture, however, resulted in the tragic death of his wife, Mary, and baby son when they perished after putting to sea in a small iron tank to avoid marauding Aborigines. The remains of the Watson's stone cottage are still evident on the island.

Lizard Island was declared a national park in 1939 and the other islands in the group added in 1987. In 1967 the Queensland government called for tenders for the lease of the island, and the Queensland-based Suncorp Finance Company gained the original lease which they still hold, theirs being the only submission to include an airstrip. In 1970, 200 years after Cook's landing, the airstrip was opened and the Company's first board meeting was held on Lizard. This was followed, in 1972, by the provision of temporary caravan accommodation which was used from 1973 by representatives of the Australian Museum, Sydney, in the establishment of their Marine Research Station, and by those involved in the planning of the Lodge, construction of which started in 1974.

The Research Station's current pamphlet accurately states:

Within a 15 mile radius of Lizard Island can be found most of the reef and island types characteristic of the entire Great Barrier Reef...It can be fairly stated that in the vicinity of Lizard Island are found an enormous number of

LIZARD ISLAND
- A Check-off List for the Travelling Fly-Fisherman

PRE-TRAVEL

See Chapter 2.

CURRENCY

See Chapter 2. All major credit cards are accepted.

TRAVEL

Cairns is an international airport servicing Asia, America and New Zealand. There are daily afternoon flights between Lizard Island and Cairns on Sunstate Airlines. The return one-class airfare is $US250. Return connections Cairns to Brisbane and Sydney are from $US230 and $US330 respectively but these costs can be reduced in package deals.

tropical marine habitats located in the richest area of the largest coral reef system in the world.

The Research Station is now world famous. It is managed locally under the auspices of the Australian Museum, Sydney, and is supported by sponsors and funded for day-to-day operations by users (universities, research scientists, budding Ph.Ds and so on), and visitors and local shop sales (70 percent); and by the Australian Museum Trust and the Lizard Island Research Foundation (30 percent). In 1994, 150 users studied at the station, working on 52 projects. Movement of fish and location of species, and study of hard corals were the two predominant marine studies, while management studies included species' commercial value (particularly coral trout), catch per unit effort (declining), and the need for regulation. The station is also an educational base for universities and schools, and television projects. It receives around 1500 visitors each year.

The Lodge was officially opened in 1975, and accommodation was gradually increased to reach optimum capacity in 1995 of 40 twin units looked after by a staff-to-guest ratio of 2:3. In 1987, Bush Pilot Airways (now Air Queensland), sold its sub-lease for the Lodge and facilities to the then Trans-Australia Airlines, now Qantas. Suncorp remains the owner of the original lease, and Qantas manages its sub-lease through its subsidiary, Australian Resorts.

Unit accommodation has air-conditioning, private bathrooms, king or twin beds, telephone and many extras. There is a central lounge with a small library, a bar and a dining area with widely spaced tables overlooking the beach. Sporting facilities include beach and pool swimming, tennis, wind-surfing, water-skiing, sailing, boat trips, snorkelling, paddle-skiing, hiking, and the provision of self-drive, aluminium dinghies.

In sporting terms, however, Lizard Island is most famous for its blue-water game fishing. Big-game fishing is the mighty draw card each year between August and December when international anglers come time and time again to pit their skills and strength against the majestic black marlin. The annual Black Marlin Classic is held in October and the Lizard Island Game Fishing Club holds a remarkable set of records: seven World, and two Australian. The Lodge is booked out during this period and management has even built a separate 'marlin facility' some distance from the Lodge which provides (in season) washing, toilet, and eating and drinking facilities for the visiting boats and their fishermen.

Apart from this, year-round light-tackle sportfishing for sailfish, mackerel, barracuda, tuna, trevally and other pelagic species is excellent and can provide reel-stripping excitement for the travelling fly-fisherman who learns quickly that this is a very different sport from stalking trout in mountain streams with lightweight gear and size 16 dry flies. Indeed, to put it in true perspective, I believe that saltwater fly-fishing should be described more accurately as saltwater streamer or lure fishing (a controversial point among the various types of salmonid anglers).

ACCOMMODATION

Unit tariffs at Lizard Island are $US360 per person per day twin share ($US515 single occupancy), for the two suites $US390 (and $US585), and for the villas $US425 (and $US620). Bookings should be made through:
  Lizard Island
  PMB40 Cairns
  Queensland 4870
  Australia
  Phone: INT. 61.(0)70.603999
  (From November 1997:
  61.(0)7.40603999)
  Fax: INT.61.(0)70.603991
  (From November 1997:
  61.(0)7.40603991)

FACILITIES

Tariff is all inclusive with the exception of shopping, laundry, telephone, drinks and game- or diving-boat charter. Game boat charter varies from $US730 to $US1120 per day depending on the season and the duration of the charter, and can be split among a number of anglers. There is a small shop at the Lodge providing chemist supplies, sunscreen, film and clothing. Two nurses are on full time duty and the Royal Flying Doctor Service is only 50 minutes distant. There is a range of free sporting facilities on the island.

TIME ZONE

The time zone in Queensland is ten hours ahead of Greenwich Mean Time and remains so throughout the year.

ELECTRICITY

Lizard Island operates on a 240 volt power supply. There are also 110 volt electric razor points are available in each unit.

CLIMATE AND CLOTHING

The climate is temperate tropical with temperatures ranging from 23°C to 32°C with high humidity. There are two distinct seasons, the wet from November through March (with occasional cyclones) and the dry from May through August. During the changeover periods the weather is unpredictable but normally moist. Summer clothing is recommended throughout the year and the lodge is informal. Don't forget your hat and sunscreen.

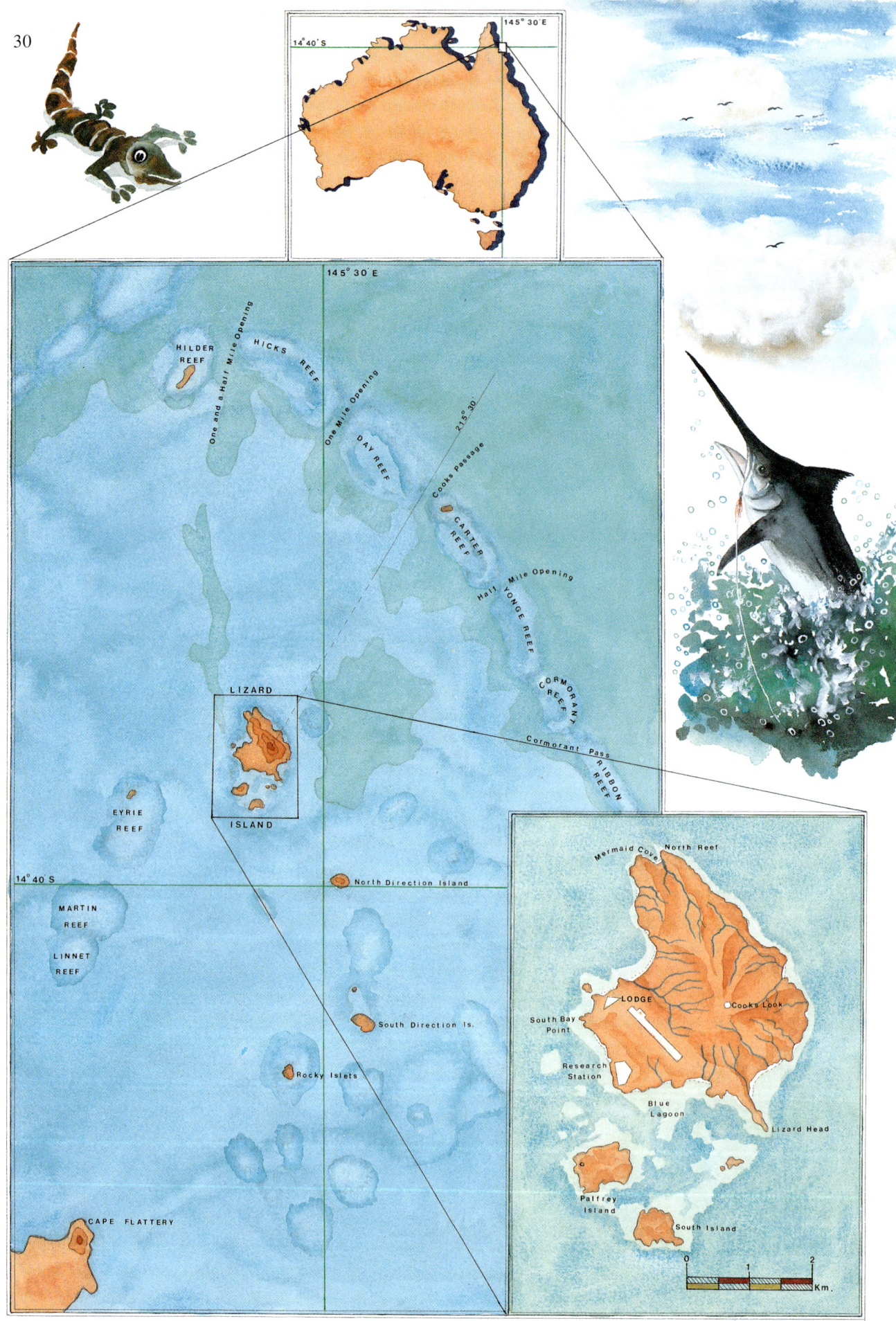

Mudmap of Lizard Island

Getting to Lizard Island

The only regular method of transport to and from Lizard Island is by the Sunstate Airlines' daily flight which leaves Cairns in the early afternoon, takes an hour to reach the island, and returns to the mainland about 15 minutes later. In the marlin season these Sunstate flights are sometimes doubled. The airstrip can also take chartered aircraft up to Cessna Citation size, but not at full load.

Cairns is an international airport with connections to Asia, America and New Zealand. For the angler approaching from the more densely populated south in Australia, there are daily flights from and to Brisbane, Sydney and Melbourne.

Accommodation

The luxurious Lodge is the only permanent visitor accommodation on Lizard Island although yachts and pleasure craft can anchor off and make use of island facilities by prior arrangement, and camping is possible in a designated site by permit obtained through the Cairns office of the Queensland National Parks and Wildlife Service. Generally, however, the Lodge and the Research Station are off-limits for non-residential guests.

Lodge tariffs are relatively expensive but are all inclusive with the exception of shopping, laundry, telephone, drinks and game- or diving-boat charter. There are 30 standard units, two suites and eight villas on Sunset Point. Occupancy rates are high and average 35 percent from Europe and 30 percent from America. Two nurses are employed full time, and the Royal Flying Doctor Service is only 50 minutes away. The island also functions effectively in the Air-Sea-Rescue organisation.

The Waters and Regulations

The waters immediately adjacent to Lizard Island are tightly regulated with extensive prohibited areas to allow unencumbered research by the

Lizard Island Lodge

Station. There are other nearby waters where fishing methods are also controlled, but none of this detracts from good fishing in other easily-accessed open areas—indeed the proliferation of fish is probably enhanced by these regulations. Prohibitions and restrictions also apply in many other areas of the Great Barrier Reef Marine Park and full details are readily available from the Lodge and the Research Station.

Fly casting and trolling (*harling*) produce good results along the reef drop-offs clockwise around the island from North Reef to Lizard Head, and from South Island to South Bay Point where both mackerel and trevally abound. This angling requires one of the self-drive, outboard-powered dinghies.

Charter of the game boat is essential to cover the outer reefs and the passages between them for those seeking more adventurous fly-fishing for sailfish, tuna and big mackerel.

Tackle and Flies

When talking about saltwater fly-fishing tackle at Lizard Island, the discussion centres around nine-foot, ten-weight (or bigger, up to 15-weight) rods, and matching reels, with velvet-smooth drag right up to lockup, that can hold up to 500 yards of 50-pound backing astern of the fly line. Also, the angler should forget about fine, tapered leaders and start thinking in terms of three or four feet of 40-pound monofilament connected to two feet of (say) 22-pound test tippet, then nine inches of wire or 80-pound shock tippet with the fly at the end. And the joining knots have to match this heavy stuff too. Lefty Kreh, in his excellent reference book *Fly-fishing in Saltwater*, describes these in detail. But, remember, once all this gear is rigged to a 650-gram shooting-head and fast-sink fly line, casting can become onerous to say the least.

Thus rigged, and using a nine-foot Loomis GLX ten-weight and System Two 10/11 reel, when I hooked my first 20-pound mackerel off the outer reefs, I found I had more to learn. The reel couldn't handle it. At maximum drag it simply unwound like a toy top, and pushed beyond maximum (which is possible but not recommended with that reel), although holding the situation in check, when the line went out it did so in abrupt jerks—a very good recipe for breakoff. I took notice of this lesson, made an indulgent phone call to the Alpine Angler in Cooma, and arranged delivery of a big Fin-Nor at my next stop. It solved the problem.

The saltwater environment can produce other hazards for the fly-fisherman. First, salt-caking and corrosion of tackle must be considered daily whether or not the angler is using corrosion-resistant materials. Take your gear into the shower with you at the end of each day, and strip and dress your lines regularly. Next, accommodation in the tropics very often includes big, ceiling fans. It may seem obvious that rods should not be rigged, tested or played with indoors unless the fan is switched off, but anglers who have had to repair or replace expensive rods in the tropics are as numerous as those who have shut car doors on trout rods in the mountains. As the Lamson said to the Loomis, 'Look up and live!' Finally, in this very incomplete list, it must be

TACKLE

Fly rods should be nine-foot and ten-weight or bigger. Matching reels of very high quality with velvet-smooth drag are essential and should be capable of carrying up to 500 yards of 50-pound backing plus a 650-gram, shooting-head, fast-sink fly line. Leaders should be tough and include a test section in between heavy monofilament, and well-proven knots must be carefully prepared and checked (this is NOT 'double-blood-and-tuck, 4X to 7X territory'). Floating lines with lesser leaders are adequate inshore. Flies should include the Sauri Fly (6/0 tandem) and the Whitebait Deceiver and the Goose Creek Deceiver (2/0 and 4/0 singles).

remembered that predators native to the tropics are another hazard. In addition to hats, polaroids, sunscreen and appropriate clothing, it is a fundamental rule, when beach or estuary fishing in the tropics, to fish in pairs, when one can watch the other's back for sharks, crocodiles or stingrays.

Flies are not available at Lizard Island so they should be pre-purchased or made. I had a selection made for me before I started my tropical travels. They were ordered through the Alpine Angler in Cooma and beautifully tied by Chris Beech of Striker Flies. The most productive included the Goose Creek and the Whitebait Deceiver for inshore work, and the Sauri Fly in the deep (examples are included in the watercolour painting). It is also of interest to point out that, while the heavy leader set-up already mentioned is very necessary in the deep, inshore fly-fishing can be undertaken more comfortably and with more chance of excitement using ten-pound monofilament leaders and smaller flies. In the deep, I think I was using tandem 6/0 hooks on the Sauri, whilst inshore with the Goose the hooks were 2/0 and sometimes smaller.

The March 1995 Visit

I flew from Canberra to Sydney at dawn on Friday 24 March, then to Cairns to catch the 1.30 pm to Lizard Island. The 1.30 was running a bit late and delivered me to the Lodge around mid afternoon. That was effectively 2700 kilometres in less than five hours flying, or from 0°C to 30°C in eight hours.

For the remainder of that day I took photographs and talked to the local staff before joining the manager, Robyn Pontynen, and other guests for a dinner of delicious reef fish, crustacea and tropical fruit, augmented by some of Australia's great white wines.

Day two was a full day in one of the dinghies and accounted for a number of small (five- to eight-pound) mackerel as I circumnavigated the island clockwise from the Lodge, stopping every now and then to fish the drop-offs. At first, such a trip can be a disconcerting experience: fishing alone on a lee shore in 15 knots of southeast trade wind, in an aluminium dinghy with a six-horsepower motor! But all the equipment at Lizard is well maintained and kept in excellent working order; 'flight plans' have to be lodged before going out, and I need not have worried. It was also a happy feeling to be seeing, once again, more orange backing than fly-line for most of the day. In fact saltwater fly-fishing has many pluses.

That night I made special arrangements with the skipper of the game boat to fish the outer reefs the next day. The game boat and the diving-boat are owned and run by Lizard Island Charters, on contract to the Lodge.

We left after breakfast and headed for Hicks and Hilder Reefs, and One and a Half Mile Opening. The plan was to search for seabird and baitfish activity, make an intercept and stop with the boat in a good position for me to cast the heavy gear. The only trouble was that we found little such activity and had to resort to an alternative plan of slowly patrolling the reefs with hookless, garfish teasers out, ready to

LEFT
The author with a shoal mackerel

RIGHT
Feeding Simon

cast a Sauri Fly between them. All a bit boring: across and down, wet fly stuff I though, until the first strike. Then, on a relatively small mackerel, I learnt the limitations of my reel. It was a good-fun day, accounting for a number of mackerel (the biggest around 20 pounds) and a few trevally. Also I caught my first longtom on a fly that day, a fish of about six pounds and a new species for my record book.

I was going to release all my fish but the skipper wanted the small ones to freeze for marlin bait, and the biggest for the Lodge. Part of the contract? On return to the moorings in the late afternoon, we 'teased up Simon', Simon being a 600-pound Queensland groper who lives by the game boat moorings and feeds on fish scraps when the boat returns each day and the fish are cleaned.

What a sight. Troy, the deckie, opened the marlin door in the transom so he could hold fish scraps about a foot above the water. I jumped into the little rubber dinghy with my Nikon to get a close-up from five feet astern; then Troy held out the first scrap. Moments later there was an almighty explosion of water. I imagined Troy was gone forever and that I would be next. But when the spray cleared, I saw Troy still kneeling in the doorway with a big smile on his face and only a half a fish head left in his hand. They asked me to hold the scrap, but I said I wanted to work my camera and, left unsaid, to retain my arm.

On Monday 27 March I joined a small party on a conducted tour of the Research Station, where I was provided with the facts and figures previously mentioned. This visit, normally run on Monday and Friday mornings is, I believe, a *must* for anglers visiting Lizard Island, particularly to learn about fish distribution, catch per unit effort, and the regulations the scientists believe are necessary to maintain fish stocks for the future. More and more of my friends are turning to the saltwater fly-fishing alternative; it could become the angling sport of the twenty-first century. And this shift is understandable when one considers that mismanagement of the southeast mainland salmonid fishery in the 1980s (being driven by the politics of appeasing the masses with little regard for conservation) stood a fair chance of terminating good stream fly-fishing in a few decades, and the only untouched alternative was the salt. (In New South Wales, however, Fisheries, through their 1995 Regulations, are addressing this problem—too little, too late? but Victoria remains uncontrolled.) In contrast, the northern saltwater fly-fishing scene, which stretches north from Fraser Island, through the Great Barrier Reef and into the Gulf of Carpentaria, west across the Cobourg Peninsula, into the Kimberley and as far as the Cocos Islands, is relatively well managed, arguably under-used, and offers a recreational fishing playground unequalled in the world, and likely to remain so if present management plans are further developed and catch-and-release becomes the norm.

I dedicated one day of my final three at Lizard Island to working, and the other two to fishing in the hope that I would be able to make one last foray to the outer reef, but this was not to be as the game boat was already chartered. I had to be content with two dinghy-days. It was during this period, fishing the Goose Creek fly, that I hooked a 15-pound mackerel. Now there are certain difficulties in playing such a fish, solo, while trying to control a dinghy at the same time. I developed a routine in the end: if there was an off-shore wind blowing I would let the boat drift while playing the fish; if the wind was blowing onshore, I would keep the motor running and roar out to sea on hook-up, letting the line out under drag until I was sufficiently far out to play the fish safely from a drifting boat. It was all a bit like Hemingway's *Old Man*, and with fish that big it is not possible to boat them without stressing the rod tip: they must either by released alongside (easier said than done) or planed into and up the beach. I am against gaffs, particularly if the fish is to be released, and nets are simply not big enough.

I left copies of my previous book with the Lodge and the Research Station, and I also presented the Lodge with a little watercolour in memory of my visit. They, in turn, gave me a wonderful visit, a Lizard Island T-shirt and a heap of memories when I left for Cairns on Friday 31 March. My next stop was to be at Seven Spirit Bay in the Northern Territory where one really would need a companion to watch one's back when fishing the beaches and the estuaries for barramundi.

On my last day on the island, I spoke to the Austrian chef, Alfred Quintus, and asked him for one of his favourite recipes. I discovered he was not only the Lizard Island chef but the Group Executive Chef responsible for kitchen policy at the other Australian Resorts' lodges at Bedarra, Great Keppel, Brampton and Lindeman islands as well. This is his recipe on the right.

And a final word about Lizard Island. At the end of his third visit to the island, English comedian Harry Secombe wrote in the visitors' book: 'If I ruled the world I'd rule it from Lizard Island.'

Whole-baked Coral Trout

1 small coral trout (scaled and cleaned)
2 spring onions (chopped)
½ cm ginger root (finely chopped)
2 limes (segmented)
2 tomatoes (chopped into cubes)
1 lemongrass stalk (finely chopped)
Butter
White wine
Seasoning

CUT the fish along the back fin, halfway down to the rib cage from behind the neck, two thirds of the way to the tail.
OPEN both sides and fill with the combined vegetables.
SPRINKLE with white wine and brush with butter.
SEASON to taste and bake for 20 minutes in moderate heat.
SERVE with Lime *Beurre Blanc*.

Lime Beurre Blanc

50 ml lime juice
100 ml white wine
375 g unsalted butter

REDUCE the lime juice and white wine by one third. On low heat gradually incorporate the butter (left at room temperature) and whisk continuously (do not overheat the sauce as it may separate).

4
SEVEN SPIRIT BAY

Lightning awakens the Earth
Thundering empowers the Earth
Rainmaking feeds the Earth
Greening is the celebration of the Earth
Windstorming enlivens the Earth
Fireraging purifies the Earth
Cloudless Blue is the waiting of the Earth

S O GO the seven seasons of the Aboriginal calendar which starts in November; and so is named Seven Spirit Bay, Gurig National Park, on the Cobourg Peninsula in Arnhem Land, at the most northerly tip of the Northern Territory of Australia.

Showering with a friend was the then adventurous expression of the 1960s, now an everyday one. Thirty years later at the Seven Spirit Bay eco-development one can still shower with a friend, even friends. Not, in this instance, golden-tressed dolly birds but beautiful bright-green tree frogs who pop out from under the water. I had one friend who regularly joined me when I washed the salt from my fly lines during my evening shower. He would jump into the shower recess and play among the coils as I stripped line into the fresh water—maybe he just liked salt?

The 2200 square kilometres of the Cobourg Peninsula are a tropical wilderness which includes extensive areas of inlets, bays, creeks, rivers and beaches. Coral reefs abound offshore and low cliffs, vine thickets, casuarinas and mangroves along the coastline give way to large inland areas of sedge plain, eucalypt forest, palms, paperbark swamps and pandanus plains. It is a natural habitat for many species of flora and fauna including the protected saltwater crocodile, but the human population, discounting visitors, is thought not to exceed 50 traditional Aboriginal landowners.

Although ranger stations with air and sea access are situated at Cape Don in the west, and at Black Point on the eastern entrance to Port Essington, other access to the area has been extremely limited and is tightly controlled. There is a four-wheel drive track from Darwin to Black Point, but this is only accessible with a permit, no more than 15 of which are issued at any one time. Primary access is therefore by sea and air and, until development of the Lodge, these numbers, too, were restricted. Thus protection of the diverse ecosystems in the area has been assured.

British colonisation was attempted at Victoria Settlement in Port Essington in 1838 but it failed after 11 years; the stone ruins are still visible today when it is hard to contemplate just how humans could have existed in that heat and humidity, dressed to the neck in red army flannel. In 1923 Cobourg Peninsula was proclaimed the first reserve for the protection of flora and fauna in northern Australia, and in 1940 Aboriginal rights in the area were recognised when part of the peninsula was reserved for the use and benefit of the Aboriginal people. In 1964, the whole of the peninsula became a wildlife sanctuary, and in 1981 it became Gurig National Park with the passing of special legislation geared towards the granting of land rights to Aborigines.

In the 1980s the traditional owners of the land sought to take control of their own affairs and become involved in a local commercial project, thereby gaining a degree of economic independence. Consequently, in 1987, the Cobourg Peninsula Sanctuary Board called for expressions of interest from developers in establishing and operating a major tourist facility at Seven Spirit Bay. In August, 1987, the group that became Seven Spirit Wilderness Proprietary Limited was selected as the preferred developer. In competition with other proposals for glittering, luxury resorts—even floating hotels—theirs was to provide a small-scale, low-impact, five-star wilderness experience that would give a totally different and uniquely enjoyable experience to the sophisticated traveller; proving that ecologically sound development was possible, and providing memorable experiences for guests with the absolute minimum effect on the environment and yielding good financial returns.

Work started, according to one brochure, in late February, 1989, and was completed in April, 1990. Quite remarkable in itself; but I was told at the Lodge that, because of bad weather, the time scale was even shorter, making the achievement even more remarkable. (In 1995 the original developers sold to the Jewel Hotels and Resorts group who continue to operate the resort in much the same manner.) Then I asked about the meaning of the Seven Spirit logo (shown on the illustration of the local flies) and was told that this, like the name, related to seasons and people. The left hand fork represents lighting, and the right hand swirl relates to people at a meeting place. And, if ever there was a meeting place totally in harmony with its surroundings it must be at Seven Spirit Bay—an opinion supported by the mass of State, national and international awards it has won in the short period from 1990.

The Seven Spirit Bay complex is quite remarkable. It consists of eight widely separated groups of three 'habitats' (as the owners call them) with their bathrooms, giving a maximum occupancy, at two per habitat, of 48.

SEVEN SPIRIT BAY
- A Check-off List for the Travelling Fly-fisherman

PRE-TRAVEL

See Chapter 2.

CURRENCY

See Chapter 2. All major credit cards are accepted.

TRAVEL

Darwin is an international airport servicing Asia and Europe. The return airfare between Darwin and Seven Spirit or Darwin and Cape Don sportfishing camp, is $US200. Return economy connections to southern cities vary from $US270 to Alice Springs to $US465 to Melbourne or Sydney, but these can be reduced in package deals.

Those bathrooms have a unique design. There are three in a hexagonal block, privately serving their three separate hexagonal habitats which stand some ten paces distant. The shower, basin, mirror, and lavatory part of each private bathroom is covered and tiled, but the remainder is open to the bush with fencing and ferns to ensure privacy, encouraging long periods of contemplation to a background chorus of frogs, birds, insects and the occasional howling dingo.

The habitats, too, are exceptional. Five sides are open to the bush through fly-screened louvres, and, on my first morning, when I awoke to see an orange orb ascending through the casuarinas, I was convinced a huge cargo helicopter had lowered me and my luxurious see-through suite straight into the middle of a tropical jungle. There is a central building with reception, lounge, bar, dining and conference room, all air-conditioned (the habitats only have and need overhead fans). It is less than 400 metres from the furthest habitat, overlooking a large free-form swimming pool surrounded by natural bush, just metres from the ocean.

Regular but optional activities at Seven Spirit include bushwalking with Aboriginal guides or naturalists, marine tours, visits to Victorian Settlement, bird watching, photography (the Lodge has its own darkroom), beachcombing (shells must be left in place), and sportfishing of world class.

For the fly-fisherman there are a number of attractions at Seven Spirit: to fish the creeks and estuaries of Trepang Bay and Port Essington for barramundi, tarpon, mangrove jack and trevally; to fish the reefs for queenfish, trevally, mackerel, barracuda and other pelagics, to fish the blue waters for billfish and tuna, or to relocate to Cape Don where the Lodge, using the rangers huts, is to set up a camp dedicated to sportfishing, with boats and guides. It is all world class and the Lodge can provide boats, tackle, guides and transport for practically every requirement.

Getting to Seven Spirit Bay

The only regular method of transport to and from Seven Spirit Bay is by Executive Air Charter flights from Darwin. These operate daily throughout the year, weather permitting. They depart from Darwin in the afternoon and from Vashon Head (Seven Spirit) in the morning to accommodate incoming and outgoing interstate and international flights servicing Darwin. The flight takes under an hour to cover the 185 kilometres and charter flights are frequently arranged for individual guest requirements. At Vashon Head (Midjari Airstrip) safari wagons provide transport to and from the Lodge, a 15-kilometre, 30-minute trip which introduces guests to the local habitat and wildlife.

Darwin is an international airport with regular connections to Asia and Europe. For the angler approaching from the more densely populated south of Australia, there are daily flights from all capital cities.

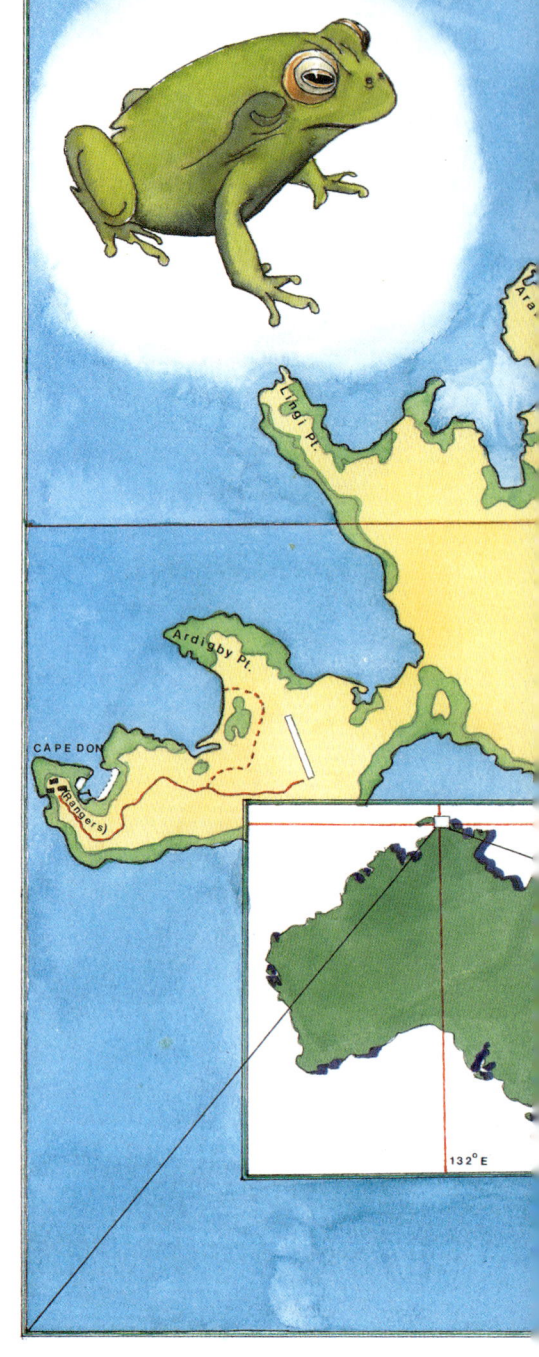

Mudmap of the Cobourg Peninsula

Accommodation

The luxurious Lodge with its habitats is the only permanent visitor accommodation on Cobourg Peninsula. The owners have a variety of rights in the area including the right to set up camps at various locations. Also the establishment of the new sportfishing facility at Cape Don as an adjunct of the Lodge is an attractive option well worthy of consideration by fly-fishermen, particularly those planning to fish with a small group of friends; it requires a minimum of two to activate and can accommodate a maximum of ten.

The Waters

The waters surrounding the Cobourg Peninsula are a veritable playground for the fly-fisherman. Whether he wants to fish for barra' and jacks in the creeks and estuaries, pelagics around the reefs, billfish in the deep, or sample the lot in a dedicated period from Cape Don, he should be truly satisfied. It should be noted, however, that access to this fishing requires boats and transport and, therefore, guides. Fishing from the local jetty is prohibited and is indifferent from the beaches. The guides under Bret Swain are first class and necessary, not only initially to help with background and methodology but also for continuing support, particularly sharp-eyed back-watching for crocodiles and other predators. They will also inform anglers of any regulations in force.

Tackle, Flies and Fishing Matters

When fishing the creeks and the estuaries, I used a nine-weight, nine-foot Hardy and a System II 10/11 reel with ten-weight floating line. Rather a heavy mismatch, nonetheless it worked well and, unless I was attempting lightweight sport, I used a 30-pound leader, doubled to the loop in the fly line, then a Bimini twist and single to the fly. I was at times sorry I had not brought my Loomis GLX five-weight with me, I knew it could handle a lot of the creek and estuary fishing even using ten- and 20-pound tippets, but I would have lost an awful lot of fish and an awful lot of the flies tied so ably by Chris Beech in Tasmania.

Around the reefs I sometimes used the same outfit but I preferred the big Loomis GLX ten-weight and Fin-Nor 4.5 with an intermediate 11-weight line, 500 yards of Tiger Braid backing and a 22-pound leader. It was silky-smooth even among the schools of frenetic queenfish up to 18 pounds.

We didn't achieve much in the deep blue where I was prepared to use this same outfit. But we once chased splashes and birds far out hoping for tuna and got trevally; and as I will report, I had 20 minutes in Port Essington connected to a 120-pound seven-gill or sleepy shark. My most successful flies inshore and in the creeks were the Pink Thing and the Barra Clouser which seemed to be equally successful around the reefs and in the deep when Harro's Deceiver and the Sauri Fly were also very effective. When the schools of queenfish became active, however, I reckon even a bare hook would have been enough.

The April 1995 Visit

After four days shut up in a hotel room in Cairns, writing the Lizard Island chapter and painting the illustrations, I wobbled out into the hot sunlight, had a haircut, picked up my processed colour transparencies and headed for Cairns airport. I caught the 5 pm flight to Darwin which, at one stage, looked like being diverted to Groote Eylandt to fuel because of cyclonic activity in Darwin, but we eventually arrived without stopping. That evening, Tuesday 4 April, a cyclone warning watch was activated as the rain poured down, and I had thoughts of sheltering for a week at Seven Spirit or of not even getting there. That

ACCOMMODATION

Habitat tariffs at Seven Spirit in the high season (April through October), are $US225 per person per day twin share ($US290 single occupancy) with reductions for children (3–16). Rates at the Cape Don Sportfishing Facility are expected to be about $US300 per person per day twin share (minimum 2, maximum 10 persons) and include dedicated guiding and fishing facilities. Bookings should be made through:
  Seven Spirit Bay
  G.P.O. Box 4721
  Darwin
  Northern Territory 0801
  Australia
  Phone: INT.61.(0)8.89790277
  Fax: INT.61.(0)8.89790284

FACILITIES

Tariff at the lodge and Cape Don is all inclusive with the exceptions of drinks, laundry, telephone/fax., and other items of a personal nature. While the Cape Don tariff includes dedicated guiding, fishing guiding at the lodge is an extra $US90 per person per day twin share. There is a small library in the conference room at the lodge. Staff are qualified in First Aid and fully equipped when engaged in activities, and a Darwin doctor is available on call.

TIME ZONE

The time zone in the Northern Territory is nine and a half hours ahead of Greenwich Mean Time and remains so throughout the year.

was the last rain I saw for a week, and next afternoon, I left the steamy heat of Darwin heading for Cobourg Peninsula in a Beechcraft Twin.

The then General Manager of the organisation that included Seven Spirit, Stephen Mitchell, was at the Lodge when I arrived and we had dinner together that evening. He provided me with much of the background to the operation, in particular about early negotiations with the Aboriginal landowners and current liaison with the five tribes under the guidance of their leader, Robert Cunningham, who lived nearby.

Creek and estuary fishing in the humidity of the tropics can be very demanding on energy, as I found the next day when Bret Swain took me to Trepang Creek for our first full day. I probably lost two or three litres of liquid, casting under the mangroves in that heat. We carried plenty of ice, soft drink and water in the tin dinghy but it was a relief to move at speed from place to place when the relative air movement felt like air-conditioning. Indeed, the final cast at any one spot was announced, more often than not, by Bret saying: 'Let's turn on the air-conditioning.'

We saw a number of barramundi but I managed to hook only one that day—a small four- or five-pounder which took the Pink Thing. I also took archer fish and trevally in the creek and counted up to eight crocodiles as we moved into the estuary and out into Trepang Bay where we took more trevally.

Day two found us operating on the western side of Port Essington, chasing trevally around Low Point, Turtle Point and False Turtle Point. This time we were operating from a Quintex runabout with a 40-horsepower outboard under clear blue skies and blistering heat. We struck good schools of trevally which seemed to like white-coloured flies—the strip retrieve has to be very fast to entice these fellows, and when they hit, they hit hard. Later, and further south in Port Essington, we were trolling flies as we moved to reach a position where we could stop for lunch and put the canopy up for shade. I had one good strike at my fly, then another, and finally weight—it felt like a trevally. But he seemed to throw the hook only to have this followed by a huge splash and much more weight. Backing left the reel faster than I can remember when, suddenly, once again the line went slack. When I started to reel in while looking over the side of the boat, I saw a big shark and several trevally. I called to Bret to have a look, whereupon the shark took off—and so did my line. Evidently, I had first hooked a trevally, the shark had followed and I had hooked him, moreover I was still connected. We planned to play him into the beach and slide him up, that was until he swam around a coral outcrop and made a nonsense of such thoughts. Bret reckoned he was a seven-gill (or sleepy) of around 120 pounds; he, too, took a Pink Thing. . .or, maybe, a bit of trevally?

Do you remember a film of the 1960s called *Ice Cold in Alex*? It was, as expected, about the Diggers in the desert campaign of the Second World War. The thing I remember most was the opening scene (where the stars and credits are given), which depicted, against a shimmering hot desert background, a tall, icy cold glass of beer, with condensation dripping down the sides to fall into the sand where it

ELECTRICITY

Seven Spirit operates on a 240-volt, generated power supply. There are also 110-volt electric-razor outlets available in each bathroom.

CLIMATE AND CLOTHING

The climate is fundamentally two-season tropical with temperatures ranging from 28°C to 32°C. The most pleasant time is May through September in the dry. March and April, and October through December are unpredictable changeover periods, and the lodge takes its own holiday during January and February in the wet season. Summer clothing is recommended throughout the year and the lodge is informal. Don't forget your hat, sunscreen and long-sleeved shirts.

TACKLE

For creek and estuary fishing, great sport is possible using five- to seven-weight outfits with ten- to 20-pound leaders. For the reefs and blue water, nine- and ten-weights (and bigger) with suitably matched reels are suitable, when leaders should start at the 20-pound mark and go upwards. I found the best flies were the Pink Thing, the Barra Clouser (both on 2/0 or 4/0 hooks), and tandem deceivers like Harro's and the Sauri Fly on 6/0s. There is little doubt that the Cobourg Peninsula is a saltwater fly-fishing playground of world class.

Harro's Deceiver.

Pink Thing.

Barra Clouser.

Saltwater flies of Seven Spirit

ABOVE
The author with a queenie (MICK REDDY)

TOP LEFT
The author into a barra' (BRETT SWAIN)

LEFT
Brett Swain at Trepang

BOTTOM LEFT
A Seven Spirit habitat

immediately evaporated. As we returned to the Lodge that afternoon the vision became a fixation until I lifted the first frosty glass of VB to my lips. As the advertisement says: 'You can get it sliding, you can get it gliding, you can get it working a plough...any old how; matter of fact, I can feel it right now. An' a hard-earned thirst deserves a big cold beer, an' the best cold beer is...' etc.

I worked all day on Saturday 8 April. Stephen kindly allowed me to setup 'studio' in the air-conditioned conference room as I find it almost impossible to work with heavy watercolour paper in the high temperatures and humidity of the tropics.

Another guide, Mick Reddy, joined me for my final two days' fishing. We concentrated mainly on Vashon Head, The Pinnacles and the blue water beyond, and Trepang Bay and its creeks and estuaries from seaward. By that stage, the water table had risen preventing the trip to Trepang by land across the peninsular. It was during this period that we struck the big schools of queenfish off The Pinnacles, hundreds of them at once, churning the water to foam as they fed on baitfish, moving quickly from location to location; very exciting stuff.

I don't think it would have mattered what fly was tied on, all that mattered was to keep ten feet of line out, race it through the water and hook up. We were using barbless hooks to allow for quick release and, with practice, four or five fish could be caught as we drifted through each school. Most were around the five-pound mark but some were well into double figures. Most days we kept two cooler-sized fish for the Lodge (I think queenfish sushimi is better than tuna). My biggest was around 12 pounds, and I thought I had hooked a monster on one occasion only to find I had foul-hooked a six-pounder in the dorsal fin.

We tried the creeks from seaward with mixed fortunes. No barramundi, but I accounted for a mixed bag of trevally, archerfish, tarpon and one good mangrove jack. We also chased what we thought would be tuna or mackerel out to sea only to find more trevally. I guess I was averaging over 30 fish each day, I was developing a swollen right wrist and incipient 'fly-caster's elbow', and almost welcomed my final day when I retired to my air-conditioned 'studio' to catch up with my notes and paintings.

I did some paintings for the Lodge and the guides and gave Bret a copy of my previous book. I also gave Nicky, who worked in the bar and dining room, a little painting of the green tree frog...and appointed her 'custodian of all green frogs at Seven Spirit'. The staff-to-guest ration there is 1:2, and I can't remember being looked after so well anywhere else by such young, enthusiastic, hard-working, friendly and competent people.

The Executive Chef, Damien Lane, provided me with his recipe for Coral Bay Numus (pickled or soused fish). It is absolutely delicious, and for those with an aversion to coriander, Damien tells me that dill can be substituted.

Coral Bay Numus

400 g queenfish or mackerel (thinly sliced)
8 lemons (juiced)
8 limes (juiced)
1 tsp minced chilli (less depending on taste)
1 tsp finely chopped lemongrass
2 tsp finely chopped coriander (or dill)
2 tsp Thai fish sauce
1 tsp cracked black pepper
1 tsp ground cumin
2 tbsp honey
1 cup julienne vegetables (carrot, leek capsicum and onion)

COMBINE all the ingredients, cover and marinate for at least two hours in the fridge.

5
EXTRAORDINARY EL QUESTRO

THE ONE-MILLION-ACRE El Questro Station, about an hour and a half's drive west of Kununurra in the Kimberley region of northern Western Australia, must be one of the world's most extraordinary fly-fishing locations. It offers angling opportunities from the cheapest to the most expensive and luxurious, with the common denominator being that barramundi are available at every level, although the greater pressures come from the greater number of anglers at the lower end of the scale and vice versa. So the best chances of big angling successes go to those few who pay more to fish the most remote areas often only accessible by helicopter—this, despite El Questro fishing management sensibly 'resting' sections of the more easily accessed areas from time to time.

El Questro was developed in the early 1990s by Englishman Will Burrell, and his Melbourne-born wife Celia. Situated on the Gibb River Road, some 100 kilometres from both Kununurra and Wyndham, it is a working cattle property improved by Will and Celia and to which they have added very extensive tourist facilities: as they say up there, 'You can run more tourists to the acre than you can cattle, and with a better economic advantage'. But cattle remain the backbone of economics in the Kimberley, and El Questro grazes some 5000, aiming to turn off 600 steers annually. These, initially, were the traditional inbred Shorthorns which Will and Celia are replacing with Brahmans to cater for the flourishing live export market into Indonesia, Malaysia and the Philippines.

At the top end of the tourist scale, super-luxury accommodation overlooking the Chamberlain River in six twin/double, air-conditioned units, with all facilities is available in Will and Celia's home, El Questro homestead. It is expensive, but not by world standards, especially when one considers the level of luxury and the inclusions of transfers, accommodation, gourmet cuisine, all beverages, and a personal itinerary and guide for the duration of the visit. The only extra cost at the homestead is for helicopter fishing or sightseeing.

EL QUESTRO
- A Check-off List for the Travelling Fly-Fisherman

PRE-TRAVEL
See Chapter 2.

CURRENCY
See Chapter 2. El Questro accepts all major credit cards.

TRAVEL
There are daily flights connecting Kununurra with Perth and Darwin. The return airfares are from $US435 and $US105 respectively. Additionally, air charters can fly direct into El Questro from Darwin or Kununurra when prices start at $US770 one way for a six-seat aeroplane ex Darwin or $US200 one way for a five-seat aeroplane ex Kununurra. Charter flights can also be arranged from Broome, Ayers Rock or Alice Springs on request.

For those using road transport, the station will provide transfers from Kununurra at $US25 per person to Emma Gorge and $US30 per person to the station. Four-wheel drive rentals at Kununurra start from $US50 per day with insurance and 100 free kilometres per day.

46

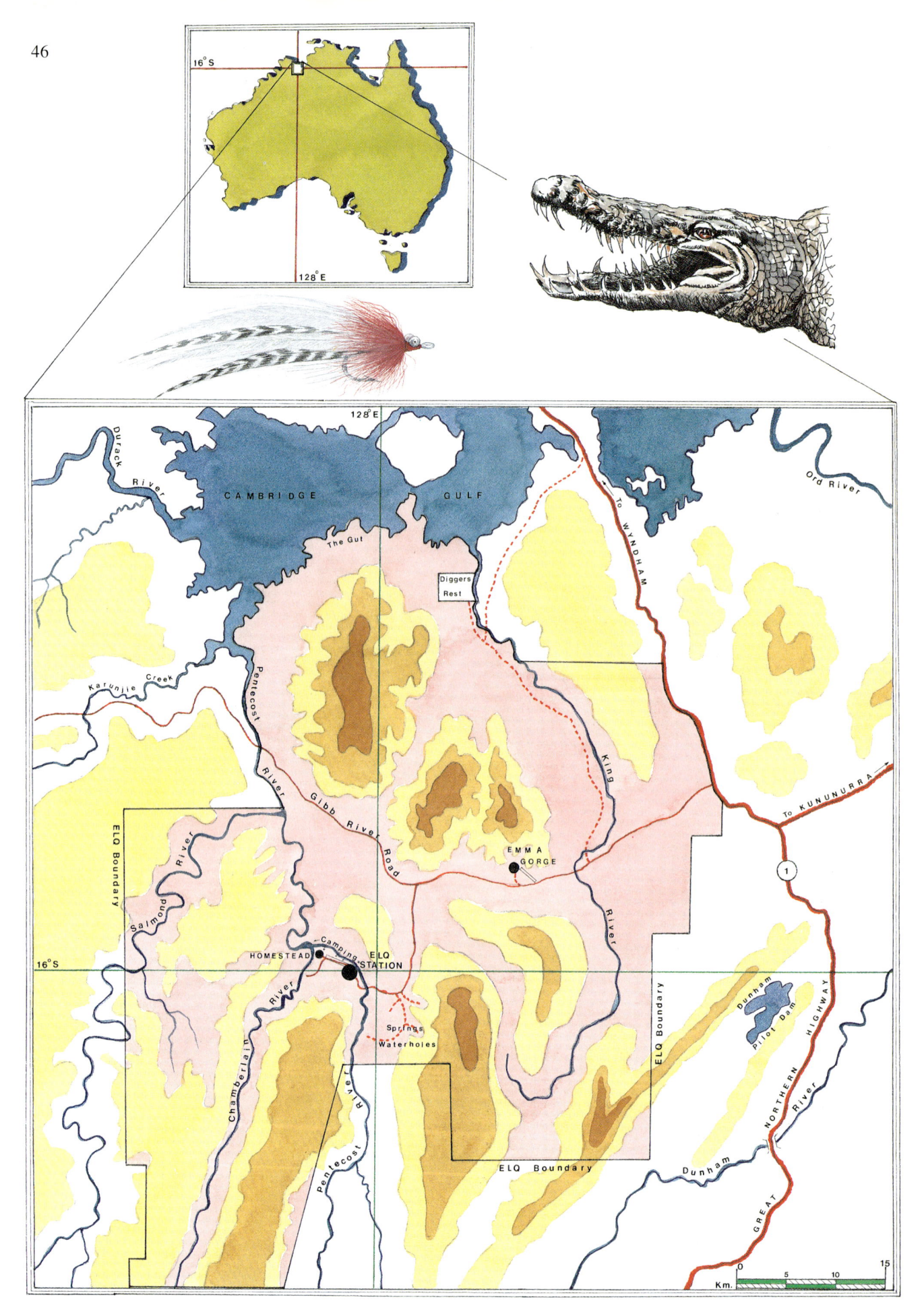

Mudmap of El Questro

Next down the scale are four air-conditioned bungalows at the heart of the Station, offering the angling adventurer great fishing combined with station life at its best. The four units have two single and two bunk beds and an en-suite bathroom each. They are serviced daily, and share a kitchen and dining/lounge overlooking the Pentecost River. Guests can make their own meals or join the cowboys, rangers and Station staff in the main mess hall. Nearby is the activities centre which includes a bar and a small shop. This is where the day's activities start and where a cold beer and lively talk and entertainment in the evening complete an exciting day's fishing. An airstrip and helicopter pad are situated literally on the doorstep.

Next, at Brumby Base, not far from the Station and overlooking the Pentecost River, there is dormitory accommodation for up to 12 people, with showers, bathroom and outback kitchen. This would be ideal for an angling group and has many inclusive features.

Then, some distance from the homestead and Station, but closer to the main highway, Emma Gorge offers quality 'tented cabin' accommodation, tropical and bush cooking, a fully licensed bar and restaurant, a large swimming pool, and its own airstrip. Fifty-eight guests can be housed in 25 twin-bedded and two family tent-cabins. There are centrally located modern bathrooms, the tents are serviced daily and 240-volt power is provided.

LEFT
El Questro barra' country

RIGHT
El Questro fishing transport

Finally, there are 26 private tent sites between the homestead and the Station overlooking the Pentecost River, all within ten minutes' drive of the store, showers, bathrooms and laundry.

Living, camping and fishing in fascinating bush surrounds, however, are not all that is offered at El Questro. Guided gorge walks among all sorts of flora and fauna, mountain-cycle riding, swimming in clear thermal springs, horse riding, four-wheel drive touring, amethyst fossicking, rock-art viewing, heli-flights and watching (or joining in) stockwork are all available. Tours can be arranged, for example to the Bungle Bungles, the Argyle Diamond Mine and the Ord River Scheme. My wife, Gini, joined me on this leg of my travels and, while I fished, wrote and painted, she travelled the area extensively, and loved every minute of it. Often we would potter together to some spot; me to fish, she to explore or to read a book under a shady tree.

El Questro is quite remarkable; yet, despite the volumes that have been written about the place in glossy magazines and shown on video tapes, one has to experience it personally to understand Will and Celia's outback dream: a dream that can be explained to the angler by pointing out that Will is a fanatical fisherman, to the non-angling visitor by referring to Celia's design and artistic talents, and to everyone who visits by observing the vital enthusiasm that this couple and their young staff exude. This is no Butlin's Holiday Camp: guests are not regimented to play 'Housie', people come to enjoy whatever they wish at a level that matches their budget. Additionally, El Questro is very eco-conscious: cars must remain on dedicated roads and tracks, campfires are allowed only in set areas, no soaps or detergents are permitted in the natural waterways, all the Station dinghies are electric powered, rubbish must be taken to the Station bins before departure, barbless hooks are the order of the day and all fish caught must be released. Warnings are given about the need to carry enough water (but not alcohol) when travelling in the outback, fauna and flora are protected, and further warnings given about crocodiles and snakes. The environmental motto at El Questro is: *Take nothing but photographs and leave nothing but footprints.*

The name El Questro almost defies description. The owners prefer the following explanation:

The name El Questro means absolutely nothing! Many versions of how the Station was named abound in the Kimberley. The version we prefer is, that the property was settled in the early 1960s, the two brothers that pegged the claim were reminded of stories about the bright red bluffs of New Mexico and the Rio Grande, thus the Spanish sounding name. A mate, we are told, who spoke Spanish handed them a translation on paper along the lines of 'land of great beauty and big mountains'. We then heard that the two hit the rum in town before they made the claim, lost the paper and came up with a Spanish name which means nothing. . .El Questro.

It is of passing trivial interest that I enjoyed this Spanish-named station as much as I enjoyed that wonderful 1992 stay in Patagonia at Estancia Huechahue—another fishing lodge with a Spanish name.

ACCOMMODATION

Riverside campsites cost $US5.50 per person/day (children under 12 years free of charge) and include access to modern bathroom facilities. Dormitory accommodation is available (max. 12 persons) at Brumby Base which includes a bathroom block and outback kitchen and dining room at an all-inclusive (tour and meals) rate of $US120 per person for two days and one night. The air-conditioned bungalows, with en suite bathrooms, linen and towels and daily service cost $US45 per day twin/share or $90 per day single occupancy. Emma Gorge 'cabin tents' are $US30 per day twin share, $US35 per day single occupancy, or $US100 per day for the family cabin. The all inclusive cost in the luxury homestead is $US470 per person/day.

El Questro Station address is:
P.O. Box 909
Banksia Street
Kununurra
Western Australia 6743
Australia
Phone: INT. 61.(0)91.691777
(From May 1997: 61.(0)8.91691777)
Fax: INT.61.(0)91.691383
(From May 1997: 61.(0)8.91691383)

FACILITIES

Kununurra is a town with full shopping, banking, restaurant, motel, medical and touring facilities. The shop at El Questro station sells basic foodstuffs, drink, toilet requirements, clothing and souvenirs; there are telephones close to all El Questro accommodation, and faxes can be arranged. Local medical services can be provided quickly.

TIME ZONE

The time zone in Western Australia is eight hours ahead of Greenwich Mean Time and remains so throughout the year.

ELECTRICITY

240 volt AC supply is available throughout El Questro.

Angling for barramundi in the Kimberley and the vast surrounding area has been a prime sport for years. At El Questro it is very good but seasonal. As I said, popular (cheaper and closer) locations come under more pressure than those more distant (and expensive), but management is sound and does much to ensure consistently good angling in all areas. Popular spots are rotated and rested, barbless hooks and catch-and-release are mandatory, pre-positioned dinghies (for four-wheel drive and helicopter access) are electric powered, and the angling manager, Jason Hamilton, has the preservation of 'his barra' at heart. So much so that I believe barra' fishing will remain good at El Questro way into the future; what is more, Jason's name and ability are well respected around the area and adjoining coast. He is remembered fondly at Seven Spirit Bay where he was once a guide, by the anglers of Darwin, and by the likes of Dean Butler who follows the game from New Guinea to Arnhem Land.

The fly-fisherman has a choice of the rivers both on and near El Questro (some are seasonal and weather dependent), and he can also venture into the brackish estuaries and out into the blue of Cambridge Gulf. It is all good, and although primarily aimed at the barra', sooty grunter, black bream, catfish and tarpon are plentiful…as are the crocodiles, both fresh and salt water, and the angler needs to keep his rear-vision mirror clear and never step into water which is not crystal clear. Also, it should be remembered that rotating helicopter blades can be even more devastating to vertically held graphite rods than overhead fans.

Getting to El Questro

El Questro's nearest major airport is at Kununurra, about 100 kilometres distant, and four-wheel drive is strongly recommended if considering the trip to and from Kununurra by car, for use while staying on the property, and particularly for touring the whole Kimberley region. Four-wheel drive vehicles are readily available at Kununurra through normal rental agencies.

There are regular domestic flights to Kununurra from Perth and Darwin connecting with all points east and south, and these capital city destinations connect with regular international flights. For those who prefer to fly all the way in, charter flights are available at varying rates from Darwin and Kununurra direct into Emma Gorge or the Station strip.

For those wishing to be collected by car from Kununurra airport, this can be arranged using Station transport at very reasonable cost.

Accommodation

There are five levels of accommodation at El Questro, ranging from the super-luxurious Lodge, through the bungalows, Brumby Base and Emma Gorge, to the private campsites. And there is no reason why the travelling angler should not try some of each. When Gini and I started our visit, a party of Victorian anglers were having their farewell breakfast at Emma Gorge restaurant and they couldn't stop smiling. The night

CLIMATE AND CLOTHING

In the wet season from November to March, temperatures can reach as high as 40°C with heavy humidity. In the cloudless months of the dry season from April through October temperatures normally reach around 30°C during the day but the nights are cool. Casual light clothing is best at all times, sneakers are suitable for fishing and good walking shoes for other activities. A hat, sunscreen and insect repellent are essential.

GUIDING

Fishing guiding is arranged by Jason Hamilton and can be booked in advance through the El Questro address, phone or fax. Prices start at $US40 per person per half day by four-wheel drive/boat (minimum 3 people), and range to $US220 per person per half day in the helicopter (2 anglers). A full day's boat fishing on the Cambridge Gulf out of Wyndham costs $US650 per boat (maximum six anglers). Conservation is the name of the game when fishing at El Questro and anglers should be prepared to fish with barbless hooks and to release all fish, (although the occasional male barra' can be kept for the table). A fishing competition for the various local species is run throughout the year with sponsored prizes ranging from holidays to fishing tackle. In the barramundi section, 12-pound gear is the maximum and the fish must be released after weighing.

TACKLE

Seven- to nine-weight outfits with suitably matched, good quality reels and upwards of 150 yards of backing are the rule for fly-fishing at El Questro. Leaders will vary depending whether the angler wants to enter the competition when he will need 12-pound test. Otherwise, I found a 20-pound double, looped to the fly line loop, and ending in a Bimini to a single tippet was ideal. The best fly for El Questro is the Pink Thing, but Yellow and Green Deceivers, and the Darwin Deceiver were also useful—sizes 2/0 to 4/0.

before they had arranged a candle-lit dinner (catered for and pre-positioned by the Station organisation) on the rocks in Chamberlain Gorge while the barra' rose. They had had two days in the bungalows, two camping, and a final fling at Emma Gorge.

The Waters

While good fishing is right alongside the campsites on the Pentecost River, this is a little distant for those staying at Emma Gorge who must travel in order to fish. Anglers have a choice of fishing that central and south part of El Questro, trying the Chamberlain, the Pentecost and the King Rivers (there are probably more crocodiles than barramundi in the King), following the Gibb River Road to the lower Pentecost crossing which is the salt/fresh changeover point, or venturing further in the dry season into the estuaries. For the more adventurous (and well-heeled), heli-fishing the upper Chamberlain and the Durack upstream from the estuary is very productive and exciting. Day trips from Wyndham to fish the Cambridge Gulf for mangrove jack, fingermark bream, and threadfin salmon can also be arranged.

Tackle Flies and Fishing Matters

I stuck to my nine-weight Hardy/System II outfit throughout my stay at El Questro. It was more than adequate for my hook-ups, and I say that in the knowledge that other guests were taking barramundi up to 25 pounds (my biggest was around ten). Like Seven Spirit, however, I had occasional thoughts about lighter gear in the creeks and estuaries, but I think one would have been hard pressed if one connected with a 20-pounder on a six-weight for example.

The best fly once again was undoubtedly the Pink Thing (2/0 or 4/0), but I had some success with Yellow and Green Deceivers and with the Darwin Deceiver. Dark flies, on the whole, were not successful (except for the Cockroach Deceiver), nor were primarily white flies: the barra' seemed to swim happily with small white archerfish in safe attendance, and I think they thought a small white fly was just another archerfish.

Casting for barra' in the Chamberlain (GINI HOLE)

EXTRAORDINARY EL QUESTRO

Cockroach Deceiver.

Pink Thing.

Yellow Deceiver.

Darwin Deceiver.

El Questro flies

The April 1995 Visit

My wife, Gini, joined me in Darwin at lunchtime on Monday 17 April and we flew out through a thunderstorm at 6 pm for the short leg to Kununurra, arriving 50 minutes later—at 5.20 pm, after the time zone change. As I've said before in my writings, these rigid time zones are crazy. The Kimberley is only just west of the Northern Territory border (where the sun rises about 6 am and sets about 6.30 pm in April) but it keeps Western Australian zone time just because it lies in the state of Western Australia. So the sun rises at about 5.00 am and sets about 5 pm. If I ran El Questro, I would keep 'El Questro Standard Time' which would be much closer to Northern Territory time than Western Australian.

At Kununurra we collected a small four-wheel drive rental car and drove to Emma Gorge where we settled into our 'tent', had a bowl of soup and an icy cold beer and retired early to see what the next day would bring. I had particularly asked the Station for air-conditioned accommodation where I could spread out my writing and painting materials; trying to handle watercolour in the tropics in high humidity is an almost impossible task. So next morning we moved into one of the air-conditioned Station bungalows where, very kindly, we were allowed to stay until the last day of our visit. I met Will Burrell for the first time that morning and he introduced me to Jason Hamilton.

Mundane tasks of life have to continue, however, even at El Questro; Gini had brought a pile of mail from down south, so I spent the rest of that first day paying the bills, getting my notes and drawings up to date, and generally making myself familiar with the area and its operations. Also, in the cool of the late afternoon, Buddy Tyson, a Station character and television star complete with white Stetson and legs so bowed you could pass a football between them, took us amethyst fossicking with some success before dinner.

On 19 and 20 April, Gini flew to the Bungle Bungles while I got down to the serious business of barramundi fishing. I started at the bottom end of the scale exploring the nearby Pentecost River on foot. Access was easy in some parts and more difficult in others, overgrown with mangroves where St Andrew's Cross spiders made their webs out of what appeared to be three-weight fly line, and where one must always keep one's eyes open for crocodiles. The Station administrative manager took me to examine a crocodile trap one morning in an area 50 metres upstream from where I'd been fishing the previous day; the trap was sprung and held a six-foot monster. Using the Pink Thing on this initial foray, I caught a number of good sooty grunter but no barramundi.

Next up the scale with Jason, I fished the Chamberlain Gorge from one of the electric-powered dinghies, but again the count was all grunters to the Pink Thing and no barra'. Then, when Gini returned from the Bungles, we drove to the Pentecost crossing on the Gibb River Road where I took two small (three pounds) barramundi, one on the Pink Thing and one on a Cockroach Deceiver (the only time a dark fly worked me for in the Kimberley).

On Friday 21 April after lunch, Gini, Jason and I took off in the helicopter and flew way upstream on the Chamberlain to a place where, in the first six casts, I hooked two barra' on the Pink Thing only to have the hook pull out both times. We flew a little downstream to a place called Jacobs Creek and I hooked a monster (12, 14...16 pounds?) first cast...and lost him too. Finally we landed at Explosion Hole where, from a pre-positioned electric-powered dinghy, I took a number of grunter and released them, then hooked my fourth barra' on a Darwin Deceiver on the last cast of the day...and lost him too.

In the last glowing rays after sunset, we climbed out of the red strata cliffs and landed back at the Station right on dark. Some might have called it a disappointing day; I thought it was a magical day even though I added $25 to my losses that evening, donating the money to the Royal Flying Doctor Service via some impromptu and private gambling.

I worked on Saturday 22 April, making notes, doing paintings for the Station, and other odds and ends. In the middle of this I took a message from Will and Celia asking us to come and stay at the homestead for our final 24 hours. So, on Sunday lunchtime, we moved up the final notch on the El Questro scale into quiet unobtrusive luxury, perched high above the Chamberlain River, surrounded by green lawns and lush tropical plants. I keep using the expression heaven on a stick, and this was just what it was.

In the afternoon, Gini, Ian (another angler) and I boarded the helicopter for a final fling way up the Durack River where a 25-pound barra' had been taken that morning. Ian, my angling mate, lost a monster lure-fishing, and I caught and released two sooty grunter and four barramundi to the Pink Thing and Darwin Deceiver. My best barra' was around ten pounds but the others were only four- or five-pounders. Again we clattered out in the exotic red, pink and orange tints of dusk and landed back at the homestead in last light.

Dinner on the balcony that evening, overlooking the floodlit gorge, was absolutely delicious (a recipe follows), and afterwards Will again demonstrated his unbounded enthusiasm for fishing by saying to me: 'Let's just go down for a flick or two before we go to bed!' And we did just that. There was, of course, an electric dinghy down the steps at the foot of the cliffs and, although we didn't land anything (I was bust by something), it was an exotic indulgence, paddling about a floodlit river in the middle of the Kimberley at midnight after what could only be described as a 6-star dinner in 6-star luxury.

We left at 8 o'clock the next morning to return the car to Kununurra, for Gini to catch a flight to Darwin and on to Sydney, and for me to fly to Perth en route to Cocos Island. It had been another remarkable visit with good fishing at an extraordinary destination.

I have made much of the various levels, costs and options at El Questro, so in choosing recipes for this chapter I have looked at both ends of the scale: Beef and Kidney Pie for the Station mess cooked by chef Kevin 'Cookie', and Seafood Fettucini cooked as part of our gourmet meal overlooking the gorge at the homestead by chef Fiona Balaam.

Beef and Kidney Pie
(Feeds a mess of about 20 people)

2 beef kidneys
3 kg beef (diced)
4 onions (diced)
6 carrots (diced)
Salt to taste

COOK together in a stew pot until the meat is tender. Thicken and place in a pie tray.

Shortcrust Pastry
5 cups plain flour
1 cup suet (taken from the kidney fat)
Pinch of salt
Water to mix

RUB the suet into the flour and add water and salt to make dough. Roll and place over pie tray. Bake until golden brown.

Seafood Fettucini
(Serves four)

Pasta
315 g plain flour
3 x 60 g eggs

BREAK eggs and mix with flour to form a dough. Knead until well blended. Pass through a pasta machine decreasing the thickness, then roll through a fettucini machine.
COOK in a large pot of boiling, salted water with a splash of oil. Cook until the pasta floats (two to three minutes).

Sauce
QUICKLY sear eight, whole baby octopus in five cloves of chopped garlic and one or two red chillies (finely chopped and without seeds). Add a cup of roughly chopped fresh scallops and cook for a further minute.

SERVING
Drain the pasta and toss with butter and a large handful of chopped Italian parsley. Stir in grated regiano and parmigiano, then add the seafood. Serve on warm plates and decorate with freshly caught *cherabin* yabbies cooked in the shell. Garnish with chopped chillies.

54

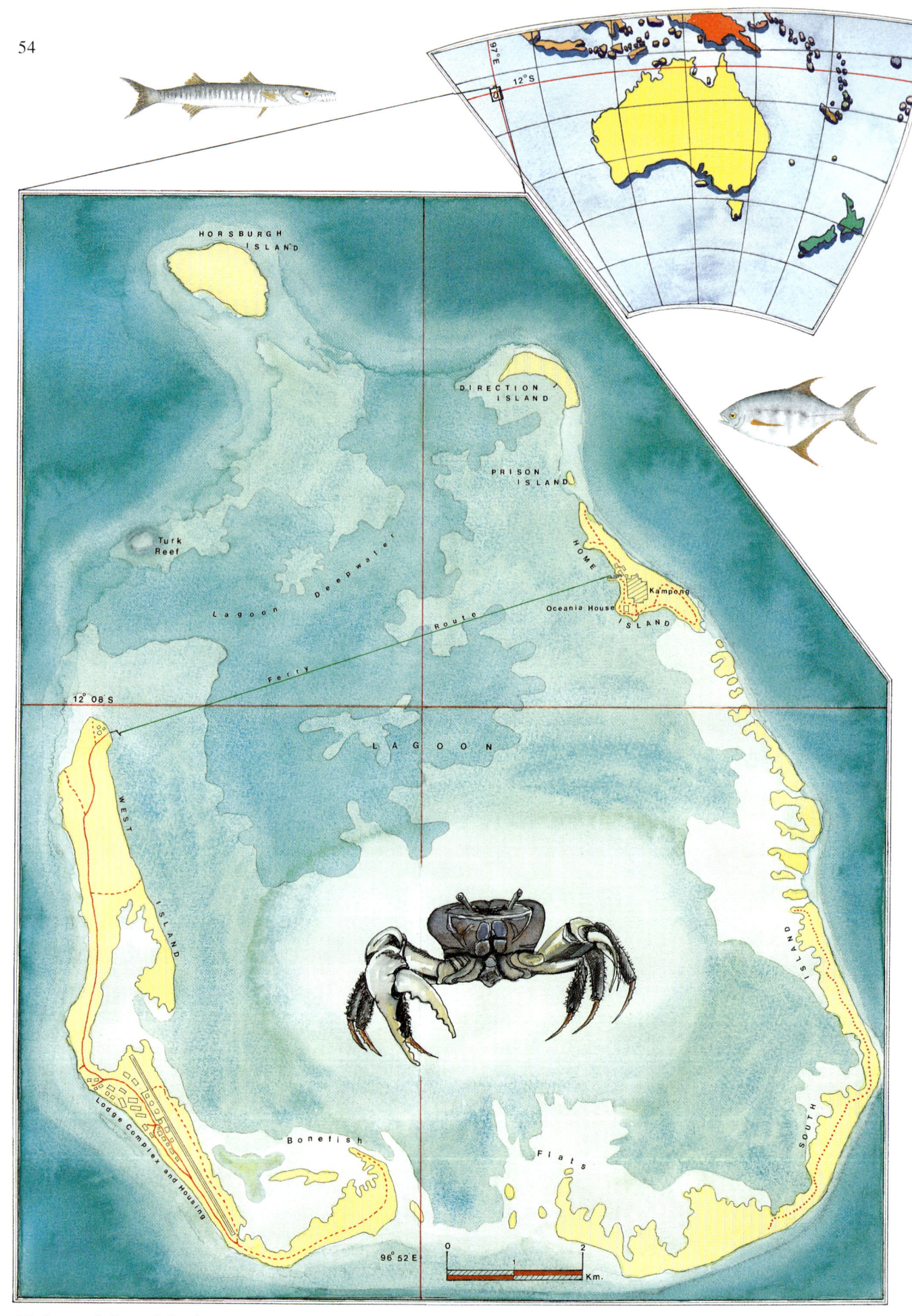

Mudmap of Cocos Island

6
THE REMOTE COCOS (KEELING) ISLANDS

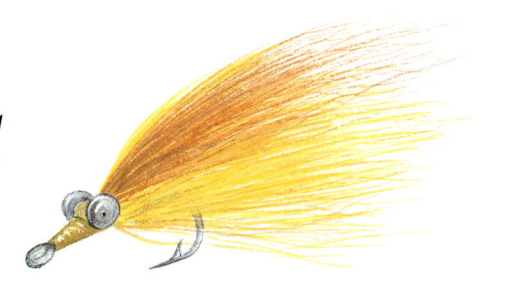

Yellow Crazy Charlie.

Sauri Fly.

Goose Creek Deceiver.

Cocos Saltwater flies

THE COCOS ISLANDS are so laid back they have almost forgotten how to yawn. So don't look for sophistication or even one-star accommodation and facilities, and be prepared to work at whatever it is you want to do: beachcombing, scuba diving, fishing, golf, volleyball, or just plain lying in the sun. If the travelling angler accepts these simplicities, he will be accommodated in adequate and clean quarters, he will eat passably well, any purchases he makes during his visit—car rentals to duty-free booze—will be relatively cheap, he can hire boats and guides to take him fishing and, above all, he will find himself surrounded by an open friendliness from the locals and a tropical lifestyle which is hard to beat.

The Cocos (Keeling) Islands are an Australian territory lying in the Indian Ocean 2800 kilometres northwest of Perth and 3700 kilometres west of Darwin; Sumatra and Java lie about 1000 kilometres northeast, and it would be hard to imagine anywhere more remote (one would therefore expect the fishing to be very good). The islands were discovered in 1609 by Captain William Keeling of the East India Company. Originally named the 'Cocos-Keeling Islands' by the British hydrographer James Horsburgh, the name was changed to the 'Cocos (Keeling) Islands' in 1955. Nowadays, most visitors refer to 'Cocos' meaning the south atoll which includes Home, West, South, Horsburgh and Direction Islands, and 'Keeling' meaning the island (of *Sydney/Emden* fame) lying 25 kilometres to the north and which is a wildlife sanctuary.

The islands were first settled in 1826 by Alexander Hare with a mixed group of less than 100 Malay-speaking Moslems whom Hare employed as slaves to harvest coconuts, produce coconut oil and tend to the fruit and vegetable patches. John Clunies-Ross, an employee of the House of Hare, arrived in 1827 and, after seven years of rivalry and friction with Hare, took control of the Home Island in 1834 after Hare died during a trip to Java and his supervisor coincidentally drowned in a mishap a little later. Despite frequent troubles with his work force and other associated problems, fortunes prospered for Clunies-Ross with the export of coconuts and coconut oil.

In 1857 the islands were annexed by Britain and for the remainder of the century, despite cyclones, riots and dysentery, the Clunies-Ross estate continued to ride a wave of prosperity, selling coconuts, copra, coconut oil and mengkudu wood to Batavia. A cable telegraph station was established in 1901 and this was supplemented by a wireless link in 1910. Suddenly, Cocos had become an important and strategic point in world communications, and in 1914 the Great War put the islands firmly on the map with the destruction of the German raider *Emden* by the Australian cruiser HMAS *Sydney* at Keeling Island.

The Second World War brought shelling from Japanese warships and air raids from Japanese-occupied Java. Allied detachments were stationed on the islands and construction of a 2000-yard metallic airstrip began on West Island towards the close of the war in 1945. The war took its toll. Leadership changed, confusion resulted, the plantation was neglected and food had to be rationed.

COCOS ISLAND
- A Check-off List for the Travelling Fly-fisherman

PRE-TRAVEL

See Chapter 2.

CURRENCY

See Chapter 2. Australian currency is used at Cocos Island and Visa, Master, and (Australian) Bank Cards are accepted.

TRAVEL

Perth is an international airport servicing Asia and Europe. Return flights to Cocos Island from Perth International Terminal are scheduled on Wednesdays and Saturdays. The return airfare is $US615. The Wednesday flight is recommended if the Cocos business shutdown is to be avoided on Saturdays. There are daily connecting flights from Perth to all other Australian capital cities.

By 1955, when Australia officially accepted the islands from the British Government, the West Island airstrip had been upgraded and became a staging point for international flights between Australia and South Africa.

In 1974 a United Nations delegation visited the islands as the result of some petty, political tub-thumping by the minister responsible at the time, and in 1978 the Australian Government negotiated the purchase of the islands, with the exception of the Clunies-Ross' family home area, from descendant John Clunies-Ross (the hyphen had been added to the family name by John Sydney C.R. in 1912). Finally, in 1984, 150 years after the establishment of the Clunies-Ross dynasty at Cocos, a United Nations mission observed an Act of Self Determination when the Cocos-Malay inhabitants voted in favour of integration with Australia.

In 1987 the copra industry was declared to be no longer profitable and the locals began to examine other ways in which to enlarge their very limited economic base. Tourism with its associated aquatic pastimes (including all types of fishing) appeared as an obvious contender, and there has been some talk since of building a casino on West Island (which I believe would be totally out of character with the islanders' lifestyle and environment). The trouble is that their laid-back attitude augurs well for nothing and badly for something. Since integration with Australia, the locals have also discovered that if one can't (won't?) work, one gets paid (the dole). And that little piece of information, in an already laid-back tropical haven, is a trigger for apathy.

Based on this background, it is no surprise that the locals view fishing as simply a means to an end: to provide food for the table. After all, subsistence fishing supplemented by rice has provided the staple diet in Malay kampongs for centuries. Skull-dragging reef fish with 100-pound gear from an anchored coracle is the name of the game at Cocos, and sportfishing wastes valuable food-collecting time. I was benevolently regarded as being slightly insane when I talked of fishing for sport, and when I started to discuss fly-fishing, they dismissed me as a madman, not a threat to their food supply.

It is an ancient and understandable attitude which could reduce lagoon fish stocks in the longer term, particularly as handline reef-fishing for the table is frequently supplemented by netting shoal fish, but I don't believe an education program, promoting conservation for the future, would be acceptable. The locals talk of 'bad times' (every ten or fifteen years), when tide, climate, algae-growth and other factors come together to 'kill' large parts of the lagoon. When this, whatever it is, happens, good table fish are seen floating belly-up in their thousands and recovery of the waters can take a number of years.

Despite this, sportfishing *is* possible at Cocos: on the flats in the lagoon for bonefish; on the flats inside the outer reef for bones and other species; in the lagoon for reef fish and pelagics, and in the blue for billfish, tuna, barracuda and wahoo. All these fish can be taken on the fly, and once my helpful locals understood this, and further understood I would either return my catch to grow bigger (for them) or give it to them for dinner, we established a very good working relationship.

ACCOMMODATION

Charges at West Island Lodge are by the room: single occupancy $US52 per night, double occupancy $US60 per night and triple occupancy $US68 per night. For deluxe rooms add $US7.50 per night. Three-bedroom houses (with linen and cooking facilities) cost $US60 per day or $US265 per week ($US300 per week if serviced twice weekly). Mini-mokes can be hired from West Island Lodge at $US30 per day. Bookings should be made through:

West Island Lodge
Phone: INT.61.(0)91.626702
(From May 1997: 61.(0)8.91626702)
Fax: INT.61.(0)91.626764
(From May 1997: 61.(0)8.91626764)

Packages (including airfares) can be arranged through:
Island Bound Holidays
214A Nicholson Road
Shenton Park
Western Australia 6008
Phone: INT.61.(0)9.3813644
(From May 1997: 61.(0)8.93813644)
Fax: INT.61.(0)9.381 2030
(From May 1997: 61.(0)8.93812030)

FACILITIES

On the West Island, all shopping and banking can be done at the supermarket. There is a post office nearby, public telephones are available, and there is a surf shop and souvenir shop in the Lodge/Airport complex. Meals are available at the Lodge mess (around $US30 per person per day), or takeaways ($US5 per person for lunch), and picnic baskets can be made up ($US10 per person). There is a medical centre in the West Island complex and nursing is on call. Low-key restaurants are also available at Home and West Island, and the West Island Club provides a bar and television (satellite) viewing.

Getting to Cocos Island

Regular flights from Perth fly in and out of Cocos on Wednesdays and Saturdays. These are known as 'Charter Days' in the Cocos and are probably the busiest days of the week with an exciting turnaround of passengers and freight. The outward flight from Perth leaves the International Terminal in the early morning, refuelling at Learmonth on the western tip of Australia (if going on from Cocos to Christmas Island), and arrives in Cocos at noon. The outgoing flight leaves Cocos 30 minutes after arrival and returns to Perth in the late afternoon, or evening if stopping at Christmas Island. For first-time visitors, the Wednesday flight is recommended because the island simply shuts down 30 minutes after the arrival of the Saturday flight and nothing much can be achieved until Monday.

Accommodation

The only available visitor accommodation at Cocos is on the West Island at West Island Lodge within easy walking distance of the airport, the Club, the supermarket and the post office. Both standard and deluxe rooms are offered for single, double and triple occupancy, and three-bedroom Lodge houses are offered on a daily or weekly basis with or without servicing. All rooms have overhead fans but it is planned to include air-conditioning in some deluxe rooms in the future.

Cars, mini-mokes, motor-scooters and bicycles can be rented through West Island Lodge.

Meals are available at the West Island Lodge mess or as take-aways. Victuals can be obtained at the supermarket, and the West Island Club, which provides a bar and television viewing area, sells hot pies over the counter. For the more adventurous, there are low-key Malay/Indian restaurants both on Home Island and in the West Island airport complex.

Ferry timetables between West and Home Islands are displayed at the Lodge reception area where there is also a souvenir shop.

GUIDING

Details of sportfishing and boat hire can be arranged through Bob Percy in Perth on:
   INT.61.(0)9.3833012
   (From May 1997: 61.(0)8.93833012).

Alternatively, Signa Knight (whose English is limited) can be contacted at Cocos on:
   INT.61.(0)91.627676
   (From May 1997: 61.(0)8.91627676).

Mardi Too can be hired at $US30 per hour. Geoff Cristie and his 'rubber ducky' can be contacted through the West Island Lodge (his charges are $US60 per day), and Dieter Gerhard, with his scuba-diving operation, can be contacted on:
   INT.61.(0)91.626580/6584
   (From May 1997: 61.(0)8.91626580/6584).

TIME ZONE

The time zone in the Cocos Islands is six and a half hours ahead of Greenwich Mean Time and remains so throughout the year.

ELECTRICITY

Cocos Island operates on 240-volt AC power supply.

Cocos Island accommodation and transport

LEFT
Beautiful Cocos Island

RIGHT
A Cocos blue trevally

The Waters

Cocos offers four different areas for the fly-fisherman. First, the tidal flats at the south end of the lagoon are best for stalking bonefish; access can be gained from the southern extremity of West Island or by boat and the fishing is best at high tide. Similar fishing is available but for bream, dart and the occasional pelagic on the flats between the beach and the reef on the seaward sides of the atoll, even directly behind the Lodge. Next, the deeper parts of the lagoon offer good fly-fishing for pelagics, and finally, the drop-offs beyond the reefs, out into the Indian Ocean, offer good opportunities for billfish, tuna, wahoo and barracuda. I also found that casting bonefish flies from the West Island jetty around high water was very productive indeed and a softly pleasant interlude after dinner in the evening.

Tackle, Flies and Fishing Matters

For fishing on the flats or from the jetty, seven- to nine- weight outfits with matching reels and floating lines with ten- to 15- pound tippets are best. But when venturing into the deeper waters of the lagoon, and certainly when fishing outside, go all the way up to ten-weights and beyond with super-smooth reels, miles of backing, sink tips and doubled 20-pound leaders twisted to a single test section, followed by a short but substantial shock tippet (I used nine-inch wire traces when the barracuda were around).

For flies I found the Crazy Charlie series was perfect for fishing the flats, with bright colours being more effective than plain whites and silvers. In the deeper water the Goose Creek Deceiver was the best fly for trevally, and the Sauri Fly was in a class of its own for anything bigger.

The May 1995 Visit

At one stage I thought my plans for Cocos would become totally unstuck. A retired naval officer and good friend, Bob Percy, who runs the best game fishing in Cocos from his boat *Mardi Too*, rang me in Darwin to say that he'd had a bad medical report and would be undergoing therapy in Perth just at the time we had planned to be in Cocos Island together. This problem was overcome in Perth when Bob and I met, and Bob arranged for his Cocos-Malay coxswain, Signa Knight, to look after me in Cocos using *Mardi Too*. But when I arrived in Cocos, Signa phoned me to explain he had just come down with chickenpox!

I nearly missed the outward flight from Perth because the hotel forgot my early call. Then I told the cab driver to rush me to the domestic terminal (I thought Cocos was part of Australia, which it is) when, in fact, the Cocos flight operates from the international terminal. And when I arrived in Cocos and had absorbed Signa's bad news, it was Saturday 29 April in the afternoon, and everything had closed down until Monday morning.

So I spent the weekend working on my El Questro notes and paintings, talking to the locals about other fishing options, forming a strategic plan of action for Monday and, in the late afternoons at high tide, fishing the flats inside the reef on the seaward side of the Lodge with success and much enjoyment. On Monday 1 May, which I didn't remember was my birthday until well into the afternoon, I hired a mini-moke for the week and explored West Island, fishing as I went. This established the Crazy Charlie flats and jetty routine, and also gave me a chance to talk to Geoff Cristie, who owns a steel-hulled 'rubber ducky', mainly used for reef fishing and diving, and who offered some advice about fishing in Cocos. That evening when we fished not far from the jetty, I saw my first two Cocos bonefish caught on lures—ten-inch minnows. I also talked with Dieter Gerhard, who runs a very popular and successful scuba-diving operation, and who told me he would also take on sportfishing to fill a market gap if he could, but was fully booked by divers.

I took the 7.30 ferry to Home Island the next morning to call on poor Signa in his sickbed (I'd had chickenpox as a child and was fortunately immune) and we made arrangements for two of his friends to take me out in their boats; one on Wednesday to fish the lagoon, and one on Friday to fish the deep blue. Before I left Home Island that day, I visited the old Clunies-Ross homestead, Oceania House, and the Cocos Museum. While the former was neglected and in sad need of repair, the latter was exceptionally well kept, interestingly presented, and a full exhibition of all the important bits of Cocos history.

Back on West Island, I took the early morning ferry to Home Island at 6.30 to join the Wednesday booking with Haji Haben, and we were

CLIMATE AND CLOTHING

The climate is fundamentally two-season tropical with temperatures ranging from 24°C to 29°C. The most pleasant period is May through September but because of the maritime influence, conditions are always reasonably comfortable. Very informal tropical clothing is recommended throughout the year. Don't forget your hat and sunscreen, and diving booties are essential for wading the flats.

TACKLE

For fishing the flats, seven- to nine-weight rods with matching reels and floating lines with ten- to 15- pound tippets are ideal. For the deep water in the lagoon and outside the reefs go up the scale to ten-weights (and bigger) with smooth-drag reels, miles of backing, sink-tip or shooting-head lines and doubled leaders with 20-pound test and shock tippet sections. I found the best flies were the Crazy Charlie series on the flats, and Goose Creek Deceivers and Sauri Flies in the deeper water and beyond the reefs.

out in the lagoon an hour later. Looking back on it I now realise it was a very funny morning and one when, from observation, I was reminded of the Islanders' requirement for subsistence fishing. The boat was a small open 'tinnie' with an adequate Yamaha on the back, but it was half-filled with plastic buckets of what looked and smelled like ten-year-old dead fish and garbage. 'Have to feed the chickens before we fish', I was told. So off we went at high speed, punching into a 15-knot southeaster, getting soaking wet, to reach one of the tiny islands between Home and South Island where Haji had a camp. . .and chickens. The one consolation was that the stench blew astern as we bashed our way into the wind.

Having fed the chickens and removed the smell, we set off to fish. 'Perhaps we could try the southern flats where Signa says there are bonefish,' I said. 'No, we anchor and catch dinner,' was the reply, and I was introduced to skull-dragging for the table. Finally, towards the end of the morning, I persuaded Haji to patrol the reefs so I could troll a Goose Creek. I would have accepted anything by then. Almost immediately I astonished my host when I hooked a good blue trevally and gave it to him (it was double the weight of his total morning's catch); his eyes rolled back in his head and he decided to return to the moorings. Two very different philosophies had met with happy results in Cocos lagoon. Indeed, it was very kind of Signa to help me from his sickbed and Haji to take me fishing.

On Thursday 4 May, I fished with Geoff Cristie from the rubber ducky. It was more skull-dragging, but skilful skull-dragging this time. The fisherman would lower his bait on a 30-pound line over the side and have another line of 80-pound test at standby, with a whole crab on an 8/0 hook. Then, wearing a face mask, he would lean over the side to watch the first bait. When it hooked something such as a two-pound bream, the hooked fish would be left pulling at depth to attract something huge while the 80-pound stuff was lowered to hook whatever that was (hopefully a big coral trout). Then, if the big fellow took the crab, frantic heaving and yelling would start in order to boat the big fish before the sharks got him. It was hardly sportfishing but side-splittingly funny at times (although taken very seriously because it was food for the Lodge mess table).

The Friday expedition started when I left at about 7.30 that morning from the West Island jetty in a small but professionally-fitted game boat (courtesy of Signa's influence). Diawa 50 game rods with Penn Senators were rigged either side, but I asked the skipper, Michael Kaulie, for one to be removed so I could operate with the fly, using the other as a teaser. We must have patrolled the outer west side of West Island for two hours or more without a touch. There was plenty of seabird and flying fish activity, the weather was perfect, but no fish.

Michael told me that although the main outer reef activity takes place from October to March, he was surprised that we didn't raise a wahoo or barracuda that day. So we headed for home with me trolling a Sauri Fly just in case. As we passed from the deep into the lagoon there was a violent explosion of water around my fly, the line shot out smoothly but very fast, and by the time I had increased the drag on the Fin-Nor to what I believed a 20-pound test section could live with, I was looking astern along 250 yards of Tiger Braid, yelling at the Michael to back up and get rid of the other bloody Diawa! Again it was a matter of experience. Had I hooked the fish on one of the Diawas, it would have been a simple matter of slugging it out. But I was using a delicate fly rod which he had never before seen used on big pelagics and had no knowledge of how the boat should be used in support.

Fifteen minutes later I had the beginning of the fly line back on the reel when the need for further education became apparent. The fish decided to circle the boat at high speed and occasionally pass directly underneath it. Keeping the rod out of the way of people, passing it from hand to hand around aerials and various other uprights, often with the tip being pulled down into the water, I managed to get the double leader to the rod tip when Michael skilfully grabbed the single 20-pound test tippet. Stupidly I had no shock tippet and *bingo*—the fish 'auto-released'.

We watched him, a barracuda estimated at four and a half feet and 30 pounds, swim slowly away with one of my favourite Sauri Flies in his mouth.

I still had not caught a bone, so on Saturday 6 May when I was due to fly out at midday, I drove at first light down to the southeast extremity of West Island to wade the flats with my old Hardy and the Crazy Charlie. Almost immediately I saw three moving shadows; I cast to their right and in front of them, and came up with a three-pound bone. They are there in the Cocos Islands, but in nothing like the proliferation at Christmas Island in the Pacific Ocean.

I flew to Perth via the Indian Ocean Christmas Island that afternoon, and home to Canberra the next day.

The first part of my southwest Pacific fly-fishing adventures had been successful, very educational, and a heck of a lot of fun. Before completing my southern journeys in October and November 1995, I was due to travel next through Russia and eastern Europe to produce a further guide to fly-fishing around the world. So on return to Canberra on 7 May, apart from completing my writings and illustrations for these early chapters, I started to concentrate on the northern hemispherian expedition to take place from June to September.

Incidentally, I tried to get a Cocos Island recipe—the chef at the West Island Lodge made a particularly delicious chocolate pudding which was unrefusable with ice cream—but it never eventuated.

I told you that Cocos Island was laid back.

7
THE GULF OF CARPENTARIA

Goose Creek Deceiver.

Pink Thing.

Thong Popper.

Flies of Carpentaria

In late September 1995, after three months of fly-fishing across Russia and eastern Europe it was a pleasure to return to the relative normalcy of Australia and fly to northern Queensland at the end of the cool dry season to join Carpentaria Seafaris for a week's saltwater fly-fishing on the west side of York Peninsula in the Gulf of Carpentaria.

My hosts, Greg and Jennifer Bethune, have wholly owned their successful private operation since early 1992. Activities are centred on *Capricorn Mist*, the 40-foot mothership, and branch out by day in three attendant outboard-motor-powered dinghies. Cairns, where Greg's father Joseph runs the booking office, is the start and finish point for this eight-day, seven-night, wilderness fishing adventure, which runs from Wednesday to Wednesday or Saturday to Saturday from April through November.

From Cairns guests are booked on the regular Flight West service to Bamaga, via Horn Island, and return direct to Cairns a week later. They are met at Bamaga airport and driven to Seisia where *Capricorn Mist* is berthed, ready to get underway with dinghies in tow around 2 p.m. when all are settled onboard. For the surveyed maximum of six guests, there are six comfortable bunks in the forward cabin and two more, if desired, in the open air of the flying bridge. The owners' cabin is aft, and there is an amply-supplied hot fresh water shower and full-size flushing loo in the little bathroom. The big and airy main cabin is superbly fitted and comfortable, there is huge refrigeration capacity and the package includes all meals (delicious), linen and towels, tackle and outboard fuel and guiding and tuition. And all of this (Cairns to Cairns) is offered at a very attractive price, the only additional charge being for alcohol which can be pre-ordered (at Cairns prices plus freight) through the booking office and provided chilled onboard.

In addition to being well appointed, *Capricorn Mist* is professionally and carefully maintained. She is slipped, surveyed and anti-fouled annually at Weipa, all machinery, lifesaving and navigation equipment is kept in good working order and high safety standards are enforced.

A typical safari leaves Seisia to proceed south down the west coast of Cape York, trolling with lures, to anchor off Vrilya Point for the first night, getting underway before dawn the next day to reach a southernmost point of operations, such as the Jackson or Skardon Rivers, by lunchtime. For the next five days, slow progress is made northwards, stopping for long periods and often overnight in the estuaries of, say, the Jackson and Doughboy Rivers to fish from the dinghies; upstream for barra' and jacks, in the river mouths and offshore for pelagics, and from the beaches for queenfish and trevally. Other streams (the MacDonald, Cotterell and Crystal) and offshore reefs might be visited later in the period, and schools of tuna chased to seaward as progress is made northwards to return to Seisia the evening before return to Cairns.

Trips can also be preplanned to cater for the special requirements of a given group; for example fly-fishing for barra', or chasing billfish off Kerr Reef which lies to the southwest of the Skardon. Whatever is chosen, Greg and Jennifer provide some of the best value for money I have experienced in the entire international angling market.

CARPENTARIA SEAFARIS
- A Check-off List for the Travelling Fly-Fisherman

PRE-TRAVEL

See Chapter 2.

CURRENCY

See Chapter 2. International telegraphic money transfers are accepted by the booking office.

TRAVEL

Cairns is an international airport servicing Asia, America and New Zealand. Return connections Cairns to Brisbane and Sydney are from $US230 and $US330 respectively but these costs can be reduced in package deals.
The return flight Cairns to Bamaga is included in the overall package cost.

Getting to Carpentaria

This is simply a matter of getting to Cairns in time for the 9.30 am flight to Bamaga and arranging departure ex-Cairns having returned from Bamaga around 2 pm a week later. Everything in between is handled in the package, and the booking office can arrange accommodation in Cairns prior to and following the safari if desired or required to make other flight connections.

Cairns is an international airport with connections to Asia, America and New Zealand. There are daily flights from and to southeastern state capitals for the angler approaching from the more densely populated south in Australia.

Accommodation

The very comfortable living conditions for a maximum of six anglers onboard *Capricorn Mist* have been described. Accommodation in Cairns, if private rather than booking-office accommodation is required, is readily available and ranges from one- to five- star quality.

The Waters, the Fish and Regulations

The waters of the area are relatively shallow, tidal and tropically warm. The rivers are clear, tea coloured and hold plenty of snags to provide shelter for barra', jacks, grunter, bream, catfish, saratoga, tarpon and mudcrabs, and the banks are overgrown with mangroves. The estuaries and beaches are significantly tidal and hold a predominance of queenfish, but trevally and ribbon fish are plentiful and the odd giant herring is a possibility. The offshore waters are clear and blue and hold big schools of northern bluefin, mackerel, queenfish, cobia and trevally, but sharks and barracuda are always lurking. The reefs are abundant in red emperor, sweetlips and coral trout, and offshore billfish activity is often reported.

Queensland Recreational Fishing Rules are readily available from Queensland Fisheries in Cairns, and Greg holds copies onboard. Additionally, Carpentaria Seafaris actively supports catch-and-release and barbless hooks, and is a member of IGFA.

In essence, this is a Mecca for the saltwater fly-fisherman, the only minor drawback being the strong southeast trade wind that blows from mid morning until sunset throughout most of the dry season.

Tackle and Flies

Six- and seven-weight outfits are fine for river, estuary and beach fishing subject to wind conditions, but nine-weights with silk-smooth reels and about 200 yards of backing are more suitable if the angler wants to carry a single general-purpose outfit. Offshore, ten- and 11-weight outfits are good, but 13-weights can cover a better spectrum especially when one considers 25- to 30-pound giant trevally and bluefin tuna.

Twelve- to 20-pound monofilament tippet is best inshore but, unlike trout fishing, it should be maximum diameter for a given test to overcome snags, rocks, coral and sharp teeth. In the blue it is best to go the whole hog: flyline to heavy tail-stopper, to 20-pound test, to 50-pound

ACCOMMODATION AND PACKAGE

Pre- and post-safari accommodation in Cairns can be booked by Carpentaria Seafaris booking office at an additional cost of around $US60 per person per day twin share. Normal hotel costs for this accommodation in Cairns start from $US75.

The cost of the all-inclusive Carpentaria Seafari package (Cairns to Cairns) is $US2050 with pre-ordered alcohol being the only extra charge. Customers are advised to carry an additional (say) $AUS100 in cash if they wish to purchase Carpentaria Seafaris' clothing (T-shirts, caps, etc.) and a video of their trip. Bookings should be made through:

Joseph A. Bethune
Carpentaria Seafaris
M.S. 1575, Malanda
Queensland 4885
Australia
Phone: INT.61.(0)70.965632
(From November 1997:
61.(0)7.40965632)
Fax: INT.61.(0)70.965151
(From November 1997:
61.(0)7.40965151)
E-Mail/Internet: Big Fish @ Internet North.COM.AU

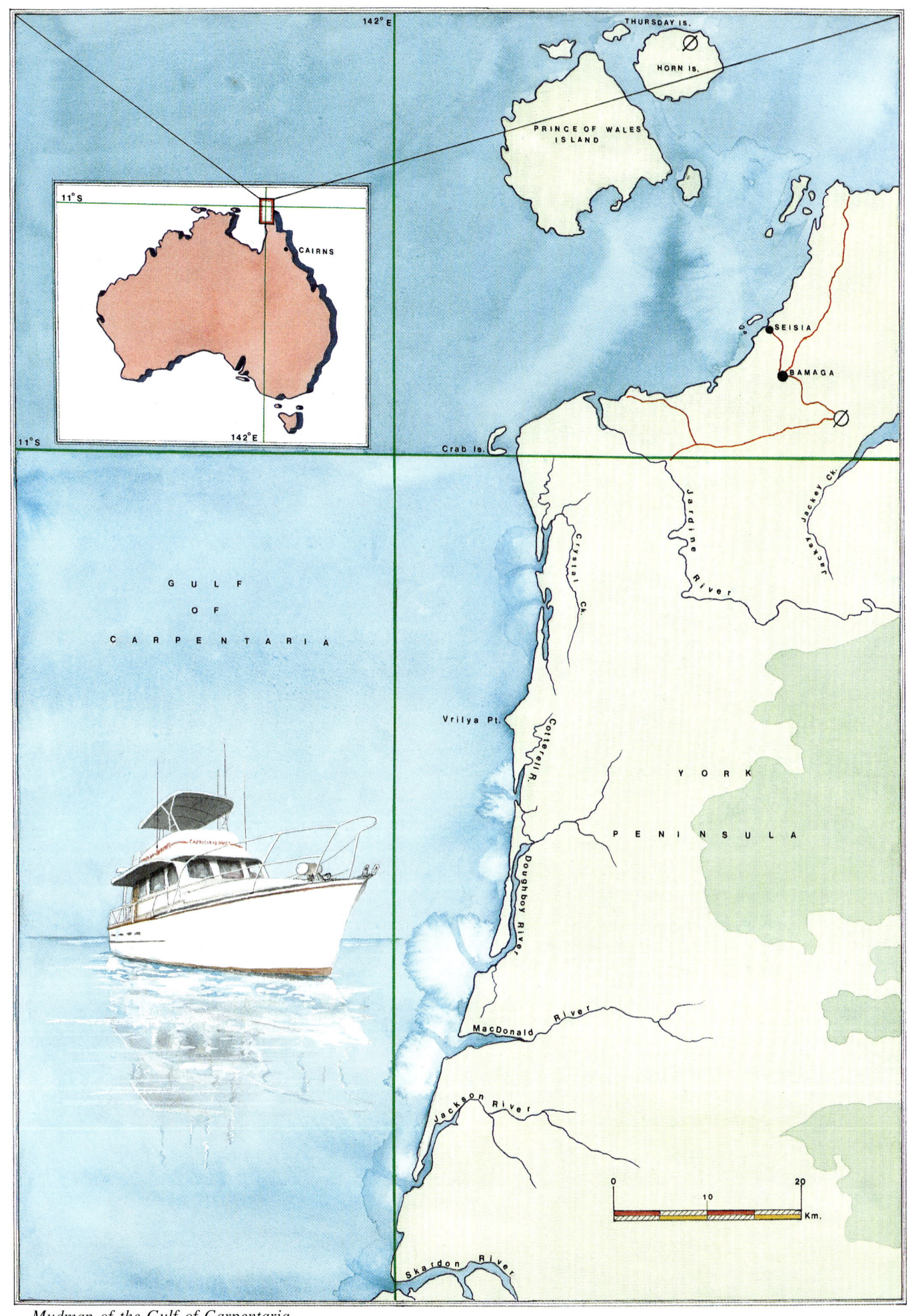

Mudmap of the Gulf of Carpentaria

shock tippet before the fly, accepting that test breakoffs will occur.

Once again, in the rivers and estuaries, the Pink Thing is probably the best fly. From the beach and also in the estuaries, small white poppers are dynamite, and the best fly in the deep water is probably the Goose Creek Deceiver.

Capricorn Mist holds a range of tackle for every preference including flies and tippet material, although most guests bring their own.

The September/October 1995 Visit

Despite hundreds of thousands of kilometres—millions even?—of flying and its accompanying airport attendance and frequent flyer privileges, I still loathe airports. Indeed the more I use them the more I hate them—the bigger the badder as far as I'm concerned. Particularly after Russia, I am convinced something will go wrong. It's not the flying, it's the baggage-handling, form-completing, petty official, customs- and immigration-regulating nightmare of herding the travelling masses like sheep that gets to me. Yet I find I spend more time in these loathsome barns to allow for contingencies before take off rather than be caught, for example, in a cab in a traffic jam two miles from the terminal with 15 minutes to go before boarding (PANIC!). I'm told it is all psychological, that everything is computerised and automatic these days, and that I should stop worrying. But it doesn't help one little schmick.

On this occasion the 6.30 am flight to Cairns via Brisbane was delayed an hour (more frequent flyer coffee and croissants), reprogrammed through Sydney, and arrived in Cairns two hours late. It didn't matter. . .but what did I tell you?

From arrival in Cairns things began to look up. The trip to Bamaga the next morning was easy, Greg met us at the airport to take us to Seisia, and I met my fishing companions for the next week. There was Vance Porter, a retired Mobil Oil man from Colorado and his son, Patrick, both keen stream fly-fishermen in the States but visiting Carpentaria Seafaris to lure- and bait-fish on the advice of a Denver newspaper article written by a friend and a previous Carpentaria Seafaris' customer.

LEFT AND RIGHT
Capricorn Mist *and the comfortable main cabin*

The fourth angler was Mitchell Phillips, a Sydney diveshop operator and keen conventional fisherman who, by the end of the trip, was talking about buying fly gear and taking lessons.

This cross-section of anglers was interesting and a lesson for those who accuse others of angling purism. We had a couple of American fly-fishermen who fished only conventionally throughout the trip, a dedicated conventional fisherman wanting to try fly-fishing in the future, and me (often accused of fly-fishing purism) being the only angler to fish all methods during the week—albeit 90 per cent with fly because I enjoy it more, but with the occasional trolled lure and some after-dinner bait-fishing for bream. Greg and I discussed this at length, and we both agreed that although we preferred fly-fishing because of its skill and challenge, we did not consider ourselves purists.

The real point being that while fishing can mean different things to different fishermen, expressions like 'purism', 'elitism' and the 'tweedy set' went out half a century ago.

We embarked in *Capricorn Mist* at Seisia, settled in and departed with dinghies in tow for passage south. After lunch that first afternoon, progress was made down the coast towards Vrilya Point with four trolls streamed, two on each side of the dinghies astern. We took turns on the frequent—often multiple—strikes, catching and releasing mackerel, tuna, trevally and cobia. It was a relaxed and easy introduction to a good-fun week, stopping only when we anchored off Vrilya Point for dinner and a short night.

Mitchell and I slept in the two open-air bunks on the flying bridge, perhaps the most comfortable way to sleep on calm tropical nights; so comfortable indeed that when we awoke to a Gulf sunrise a little before six o'clock, we hadn't realised we had been under way for well over an hour.

Breakfast and more trolling put us in the mouth of the Jackson River with two hours to spare before lunch. Having anchored, and we stayed for three days, Greg briefed us on dinghy operations, and Mitchell and I took a boat to have a look at the estuary. He was casting lures and poppers very successfully, and I was fishing sunken saltwater flies, less successfully. We accounted for a few queenies and ribbon fish (nasty teeth) before lunch.

Over the meal we established a sort of *ad hoc* routine for the next few days: who wants to do what this afternoon? Or, at breakfast: who wants...this morning? Plans were made, people would team up to chase barra' inshore or pelagics in the deep, and the whole thing became comfortable, flexible and highly enjoyable. On the first afternoon in the Jackson, the other guests took a boat upstream to chase barra' while Greg and I took a boatload of crabpots into the Skardon. We also patrolled the coast inshore to suss out the action and were rewarded by many sightings of trevally and queenfish before Greg turned one corner too hard and I was thrown from my spotting platform gracefully into the aquamarine blue. I was back onboard before you could say 'knife'—I'd seen some of the inhabitants of the blue, and that is why during the trip none of us went swimming (voluntarily).

FACILITIES
Full living facilities including towels and linen are provided onboard *Capricorn Mist*. Radio telephone is also available and, in an emergency, MEDEVAC can be arranged quickly.

TIME ZONE
The time zone in Queensland is ten hours ahead of Greenwich Mean Time and remains so throughout the year.

ELECTRICITY
240 volt power supply is available onboard *Capricorn Mist*.

CLIMATE AND CLOTHING
The climate is temperate tropical with temperatures ranging from 20°C to 30°C, but Cape York is surprisingly mild by comparison with other tropical fishing areas in the same latitudes. Summer fishing clothing is recommended throughout (taking three or more changes as, other than dunking in a bucket of freshwater, there are no dedicated laundry facilities onboard). Because of the type of fishing, footwear is not needed, and the lifestyle is very informal—a clean T-shirt and shorts after a shower in the evening is all that is required for dinner. Don't forget your hat and sunscreen.

Fly-fishing from the beach at sunset that evening, on the way back to the boat, hooked me on Carpentaria forever. The water was flat, the sky orange turning to deep evening indigo, Greg and I were taking a fish every ten minutes, and it was one of those rare occasions when the angler just sighs with contentment. We were using small blue-tailed poppers that Greg had made from discarded thong sandals—they were dynamite.

The wildlife in that part of Australia is an additional complement. Pelicans in their thousands patrol the tidal flats, scooping crustacea and baitfish for dinner, crocodile tracks are ever present on the beaches, seagulls fight over scraps, turtles leave their slow-motion footprints and eggs in the sand, crabs creep sideways through the mangroves, oyster catchers dive-bomb baitfish, sharp-eyed falcons devour whatever is left, and big fish demolish the small—a tropical paradox of a dog-eat-dog and let-the-biggest-predator-win existence.

The most beautiful of all these exotic creatures must be the rays. The stingrays, lying placid underwater in the sand, leaving (with a very visible puff of grit) their signature as an imprint on the ocean floor when disturbed and, more evident, the magestic manta, when it climbs out of the water into the blue in search of flying fish. A video-camera, even in the most practised hands, could never get all this together—natural art inevitably outshines mankind's most professional attempts.

And, a little like the feeling in the Maniototo of New Zealand, I found there was more to fly-fishing in the Gulf of Carpentaria than just catching fish. I don't remember anyone searching for plaster of Paris, but I do rember soft tropical nights, contentment after a good day's fishing, and an enjoyment of life (even work) which comes from familiar involvement.

So the days and nights continued. Often two dinghies would fish the deep, when Vance outfished everyone and we had enormous enjoyment. Greg recovered the crabpots and we had an epoch-making dinner of chilli mudcrab one evening (recipe on page 71). Mitchell and Patrick chased the barra' from dawn to dusk with some success; every now and then I would stop for several hours to get my notes and sketches up to date, and we would gather back onboard after sunset each evening to sip a cold one, eat a delicious dinner and drop, quite contented, early into bed.

On Sunday 1 October we moved north to anchor in the mouth of the Doughboy River and continue this idyllic existence; Greg joining me upstream barra' chasing on the first afternoon, but we scored only jacks and one grunter.

I worked at the dining table in the main cabin the next morning but that evening, as the tide rose over the sandflats at the river mouth, I took a dinghy to chase the incoming trevally. It was heaps of fun spotting and casting to these ten-pounders in less than two feet of water as they chased baitfish on the incoming tide.

On our final full day in *Capricorn Mist* we weighed anchor and proceeded slowly up the coast towards Vrilya Point. Mitchell, Vance

TACKLE

While Greg holds a full range of tackle onboard, most fly-fishermen like to bring their own. I would suggest two outfits: An eight- or nine-foot, eight- or nine-weight outfit with matching good quality reel, 200 yards of 50-pound backing and a WF fly line; and a 12- to 15-weight Mega outfit with super smooth reel, up to 500 yards of 50-pound backing and a sink-tip fly line. Leaders can be made up to suit the occasion but it is worth including 15-pound, 20-pound, 30-pound and 50-pound good quality mono and some wire in your tackle bag.

For flies, a range of small light-coloured poppers with blue and green tails is essential. Pink Things 2/0 to 4/0 are best for river and estuary, and Goose Creeks 2/0 to 6/0 are the thing for the deep.

Don't forget good quality sunglasses (and if you are into photography a variable polaroid filter is a must—but take off your sunglasses when you make adjustments).

Greg (l) and Vance (r) with a nice G.T.

and Patrick took one dinghy to chase barra' in the Cotterell and I took another to chase bluefin tuna in the blue. We all agreed to rendezvous with the mothership in the early afternoon for the final passage to Seisia.

Hundreds of schools of bluefin were chasing baitfish in the deep; thousands of fish in any square kilometre, and probably millions from horizon to horizon. I was using Loomis rods: a nine-foot GLX ten-weight with a System II reel and ten-weight Orvis WF line, and a nine-foot IMX Mega 12/13 with a Fin-Nor 4.5 and a 13-weight Ultra line.

At first I tried the stealthy approach, creeping up on the school, as for trout. But this didn't work, the fish had too much time in which to sense my presence and become spooked by the outboard motor. So I developed what was to become the sure-fire alternative: prepare the gear and strip some 20 yards of line clear and ready to cast; sight a school of fish; go flat out into the centre, cut the motor and start casting like crazy. It worked every time and accounted for some ten hookups and eight fish that morning, all to the Chris Beech-tied Goose Creek Deceiver and all around the ten- to 15-pound mark.

But there was one monster. I hooked him on the GLX ten-weight but didn't see him for the first 15 minutes even though I kept chasing the backing with the boat. After 30 minutes I'd played him out and had him near to the dinghy—roughly 25 pounds I reckoned. I had no gaff and wasn't prepared to put a huge vertical strain on a nine foot graphite rod to boat him (it is one of the easiest ways to break these rods). So, as the beach was relatively close, I thought I would steam inshore, beach him and take some photographs prior to release.

Fifty metres from the beach, with the fish 15 or 20 feet from the port quarter, I twitched to something in the peripheral vision of my left eye. Swinging round to investigate I was confronted by a brown dorsal fin, longer than my forearm, pushing up a huge bow wave as it hurtled towards my tuna. I have never felt so helpless and now have some feeling for what it must be like to be charged by a shark. It was all over in less than three seconds. The 15-foot whaler hit the tuna like a ton of bricks, rolled as 'dinner' disappeared down his mouth, and took off into the blue. Goodbye to a good tuna, one Goose Creek and ten inches of 50-pound shock tippet.

I've been involved without particular thought with fish and sharks on countless occasions before, but this was close-up action and very, very horrifying. The shark was about the same size as the dinghy and, for one horrible moment, I thought I might be on the menu for dessert.

Somewhat shakily, I made the rendezvous. The others had a successful barra' expedition, and Greg had taken a bonito on the fly from the mothership. And so northwards to moor off Seisia at sunset for a final dinner and champagne.

As we disembarked and drove to Bamaga airport the next morning, I pondered on the past week. I had fished in an exciting environment under very comfortable conditions and professional management with fellow anglers who, I am certain given the choice, would return again and again. My American friends simply couldn't believe how we in Australia could provide such perfect, virgin, pristine fishing without boats charging and hardware being hurled in every direction. I understand this and, while acknowledging that as such wilderness fishing draws more internationals and the resource comes under increasing pressure, the tight conservation and safety measures of Carpentaria Seafaris will help to protect it. Greg and Jennifer's relaxed organisation should attract considerable overseas economic input. This is good and they deserve it.

Chilli Mud Crab
(For four)

4 green mudcrabs (cleaned and cracked for eating)
2 tbsp finely chopped garlic
2 tbsp grated green ginger
½ tbsp chopped fresh chilli (to taste)
½ cup sweet sherry
½ cup chicken stock
¼ cup soy sauce
½ cup water
1 tbsp cornflour
2 tbsp sugar
1 cup eschalots (coarsely chopped)
½ cup chopped red capsicum
1 tbsp cooking oil
Dash sesame oil

PLACE the oils, garlic, ginger and chilli in a wok and saute for two minutes. Add the crabs and toss until the shells become reddish. Add the sherry, stock, soy, water and sugar; cover and steam for eight to ten minutes. Add the cornflour, eschalots and capsicum; and toss until the sauce thickens.
SERVE with hot, fresh bread.

(Greg always cooks in the Weber barbecue at the stern of *Capricorn Mist*—in this instance resting the wok inside the Weber.)

8
SALTWATER FLY-FISHING FOR BIG GAME

Before proceeding to the final chapters of this book, which cover exotic big-game fisheries, the whole business of saltwater fly rodding for big-game—marlin, sailfish, tuna and others—needs to be put into perspective and understood. In earlier chapters, the problems facing even the most experienced trout angler when taking the first step of switching to saltwater fly-fishing for pelagics—inadequate tackle, knots and practices—are evident, and I hope the naïveté of my own transition is apparent in my writing because it explains, better than any other way, the need to learn and adapt.

The second step from, say, the 30-pound class to chasing fish in excess of 50 pounds—even way up to 200 or more—is a gigantic leap. Lefty Kreh explains some of it in his *Fly Fishing in Salt Water*, the premier reference for any angler contemplating this transition, and Kaj Busch said a mouthful in his regular column in the summer 1995 issue of the magazine *Fly Life* when, writing about the need to test tackle to destruction, he said: '. . .the more lines you break in the lounge room, the less you break on the water!'

Dean Butler, colourfully known as 'Indiana' Butler, an experienced saltwater fly-fisherman whose place is in Chapter 10, works to the philosophy that only one of two factors should be allowed to give in after he hooks a big fish on the fly: the fish or the class tippet. In other words he is saying that, because the odds are stacked so heavily in favour of the fish, the angler must do everything in his power to ensure that all factors within his control—rods, reels, backing, fly lines, leaders, knots, joiners, flies and technique—are faultless. And Dean has been known to sum up by saying that the transition from trout fishing to chasing billfish with a fly is like parking the VW Beetle and jumping into a Formula One racing car.

Just as there are many proud VW Beetle owners who would never dream of driving an F1 Ferrari, however, so there are dedicated trout anglers who will not switch to the salt, let alone chase billfish with the fly. Indeed, there are many who consider that such fishing is not fly-fishing at all, and maybe they are correct. 'Casting' foot-long streamers at 'teased-up' billfish with mega gear can hardly be equated to the delicacy of presenting a tiny artificial dun to a sipping trout. Nonetheless, because of basic parallels in tackle and technique, 'saltwater fly-fishing' has become the *de facto* term for this sport, which is well worth a shot even at the family-sedan end of the scale. Lefty Kreh put it neatly when he wrote: 'I have never met a single fisherman who did not prefer a fly rod to any other type of tackle', and, 'You need not justify the lure of saltwater fly rodding to those who have tried it'. I would add that I thoroughly enjoy both types but seldom seem to have the wherewithal for a Ferrari when I park the VW.

However, the fact remains that less than a handful of anglers have landed billfish in excess of 150 pounds on the fly. Sure, a few more have hooked and played monsters (up to 400 pounds), but they haven't landed them. In two recorded instances, famous anglers had to cut and run after four hours' fighting when darkness descended and their boat had to return to base (in one case the angler even offered to buy the boat in order to continue but the offer was refused).

The odds against landing a fly-hooked fish in excess of 150 pounds are horrifyingly long. Those who chase this elusive 'holy grail' agree that, if on each day on the fishing grounds they average one fish attracted to the teasers, they are doing well. Furthermore, for each 20 fish attracted behind the boat, only ten achieve a position in which they can be cast to; half of those may be hooked, and possibly only one landed. A one-in-twenty chance of landing a big fly-caught fish in three weeks fishing! Yet, when you see your first 200-pound marlin, as he switches from the last teaser, and goes for your fly, it is (like visible trout fishing) unbelievably exciting...but the exhilaration is multiplied a hundredfold.

These are much, much greater odds than those for trout fishing and when one considers the cost of hiring a suitable game boat with an experienced crew (after already spending a small fortune on tackle), time on the water will inevitably be constrained by costs and the lengthened odds. The competent saltwater fly-fisherman with the correct, well-maintained tackle and good support will, one day, achieve the 300-pound goal. His time on the water (or available finance—the same thing whichever way you look at it) will, however, be as important as his luck.

Let us therefore return to those tackle factors within our control and examine them individually.

Rods

Because of the primary need to cast heavy gear in the saltwater environment and the other requirement to play big fish with adequate tackle, top-quality fly rods in the 12/13, 13/15 or 15/17 weight categories are essential. Many argue that 13- to 15-weights are best because they are strong enough to ensure that the class tippet will break well before the rod, yet they are not too big and heavy to inhibit accurate casting.

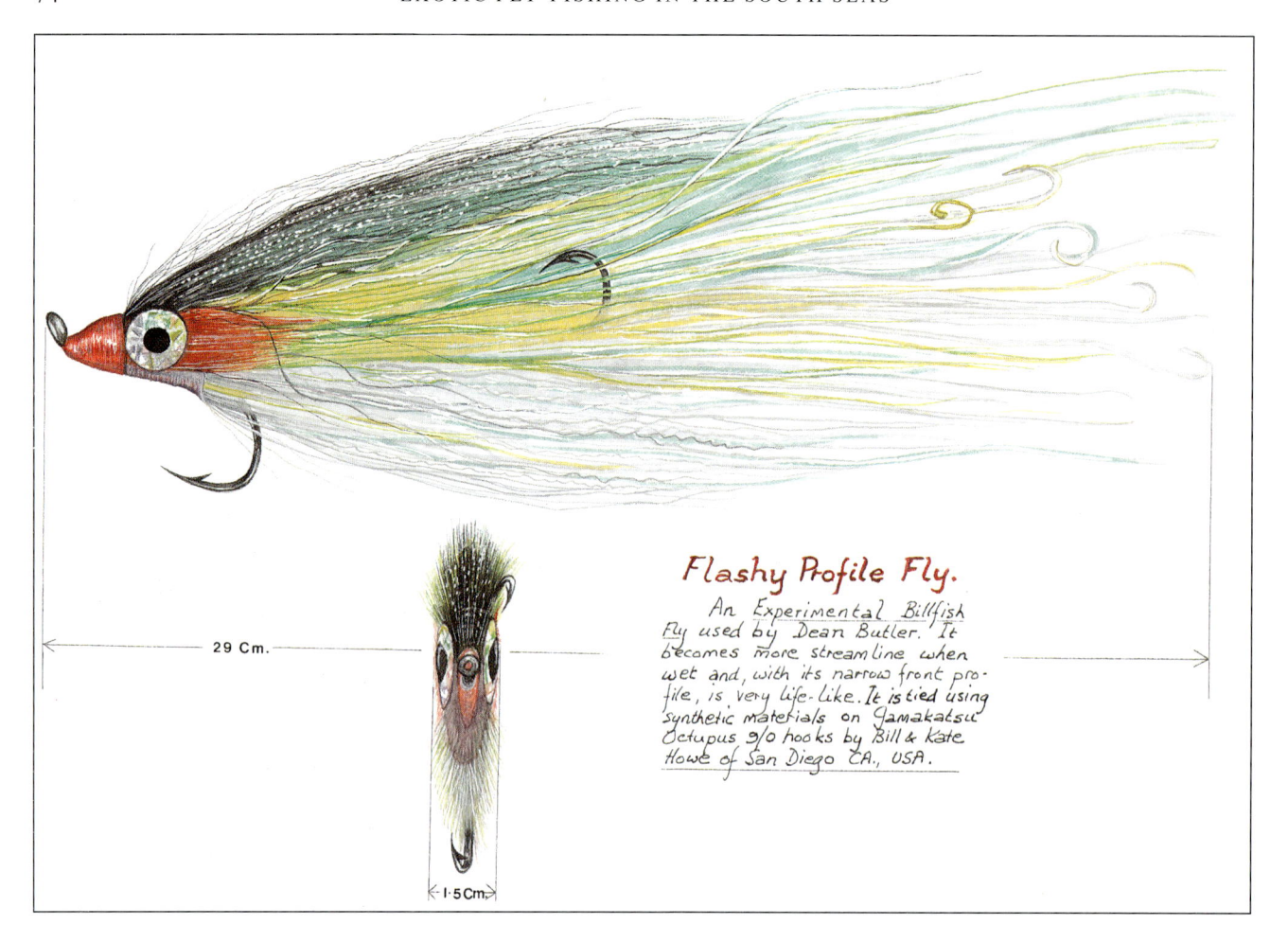

Flashy Profile Fly.
An Experimental Billfish Fly used by Dean Butler. It becomes more streamline when wet and, with its narrow front profile, is very life-like. It is tied using synthetic materials on Gamakatsu Octopus 9/0 hooks by Bill & Kate Howe of San Diego CA., USA.

Both the Loomis (IMX Mega series and the GL3) and the Sage (RPLX series) are very suitable and come with regulation fighting butts and midsections in those weights.

Reels

In terms of purchased tackle, the reel is probably the single most important piece of equipment in big-game fly-fishing. The fight, after all, is conducted from the reel so it must be of such quality as never to put additional or sudden strain on other angler-controlled components during the battle. As well as matching the rod, it is also necessary for the reel to hold up to 800 yards of backing and a 100-foot heavy fly line. The drag system must be super-smooth and slowly adjustable over a wide range; any sticking and jerking will be transferred to the rod and the class tippet, with predictable results. Strength of construction is an important factor in the rough saltwater environment, and many argue that the fewer the moving parts the better the reel. It is also important that the design of the spool should allow a fast recovery speed out to 200 yards. Both Abel and Fin-Nor make excellent '4.5' and '5' reels that meet these requirements and both offer anti-reverse options.

Backing

Gel-spun backing can be expensive (what about the rod and reel, you may well ask), but in a total of 700 yards of backing it need not all come from the top shelf. For example the first 500 yards from the reel arbor can be 30-pound waxed Micron which is cheaper and fills the reel more quickly because it is thicker. Two hundred yards of expensive 50-pound gel-spun backing can then be added, which, because it is superfine, will still leave enough space for the fly line and bits and pieces. This rig has the additional advantage that, with most action taking place out to 200 yards, recovery can be fast because the reel is always more than 75 per cent filled. Some go further and add 100 feet of 50-pound monofilament between the backing and the fly line to act as a shock-absorber against a jumping fish.

Lines

In big-game fly-fishing it should be remembered that it is still the line that takes the fly to the target and drops it to the required depth. In this instance, however, we are talking about a foot-long streamer being quickly substituted for a teaser, 40 feet astern of the boat, below the surface. We need to get this weighty attraction out and down in a matter of seconds, hence the need for 13- to 15-weight good quality lines. To achieve the distance, WF or shooting heads are required, and to get the fly down into the water a sink capability is also needed. Both styles are readily available on the market in varying weights and sinking rates. With shooting heads, some anglers add a thin fly line before the backing, others use braided gel-spun, while others again go direct to the backing or the jump-absorber. Only with instruction and experience will the angler decide exactly which combination he needs for a particular type of game fishing.

Connections, Knots, Joiners and Leaders

Thus far, and provided the angler maintains his tackle, if anything goes

New Guinea sunset

wrong, he can probably blame the manufacturer. When it comes to the connections, however, the angler is entirely on his own. The following is a Dean Butler rig from spool to fly which has stood the test of big fish over time:

a. *Backing to Reel:* Take two turns of the backing around the spool abor and secure with a uni-knot pulled tight.
b. *Backing to Fly Line:* Make a Bimini twist in the outer end of the backing, then use the loop so formed to make a three-turn surgeon's loop to give a four-braided loop. Splice the first six-inch section of a foot of 50-pound Gudebrod braided butt leader into a loop, wrap-finish the splice with fly-tying silk and seal with nail varnish. Feed the inner end of the fly line six inches into the non-loop end of the Gudebrod, wrap-finish and varnish. Now join the two loops, loop-to-loop.
c. *Fly Line to Leader Butt Section:* Fit a 50-pound Gudebrod braided butt leader loop to the outer end of the fly line in exactly the same way as the inner end (above). Using three to four feet of 60- to 80-pound Jinkai monofilament, make a non-slip-loop knot (four turns) at each end. Now join the fly line loop to the butt loop, loop-to-loop.
d. *Butt to Class Tippet:* (Class tippet maximum test: 22 pounds; minimum length measured inside the connecting knots: 15 inches). At each end of the class tippet make a Bimini twist, maintaining the minimum length between knots. On the inner end, use the loop so formed to make a three-turn surgeon's loop. Join the butt to the class tippet, loop-to-loop.
e. *Class Tippet to Shock Tippet to Fly:* (maximum shock tippet length: 12 inches, measured from the eye of the hook to the single strand of class tippet). Around the outer, two-strand loop of the doubled class tippet, just beyond the Bimini twist, make a nail knot with 80- to 200-pound monofilament; pull this knot tight against the Bimini and lock with five half hitches of doubled line around the shock tippet, then finish with a seven- or eight-turn barrel-rolled knot. This is known as the Australian Connection. With a crimp loosely inserted, pass the outer end of the shock tippet through the eye of the fly, check to ensure regulation length, pass back through the crimp and crimp tight.

Flies

As with other forms of fly-fishing, experiments are continuing to produce an effective billfish fly. The controlling factors are the requirement for the artificial to closely resemble the live teaser in size, shape, colour and movement, and for it to sink quickly but to keep a low weight-to-size ratio to help casting. An example of an effective fly is given in the diagram in this chapter, and another in Chapter 9.

Teasing

The aim of teasing is to attract a big fish to a position where it is possible to cast to it with a fly. More about this appears in Chapter 10.

Those adept at this subterfuge are in general agreement that better results are achieved with live teasers rather than hookless lures, probably due to taste and smell. In Vanuatu, however, the only marlin sighted in two days came at three hookless lures and switched to the fly within 30 feet of the transom. The experts also agree that the number of teasers (if multiple teasers are to be used) must not be more than the number of experienced people available to handle them. When a billfish is sighted it can move quickly from teaser to teaser as they are withdrawn until the fly is substituted, and one person is fully occupied on each during a period which can best be described as very exciting orchestrated chaos. Other than that, opinions and ideas about rigs and methods vary considerably; some use custom-built teaser rods with monofilament down the interior (to prevent tangles when whip-retrieved), others use conventional 50 and 80 game rigs, others again use the outrigger poles, and many combine some or all of these methods. It is best for the transitional angler to learn from watching those who have done it before, then to experiment with his own ideas.

If the fly-fisherman wants to make this extraordinary step to big-game fly-rodding, or even just to give it a go, he would be well advised to follow these principles and could do a lot worse than select New Guinea to learn the business, and both New Guinea and Vanuatu to have a go as the final two chapters explain. In the end, and above all else, he should set out to enjoy his fishing and this he will do in these stunningly beautiful parts of the Antipodes.

9
THE ISLAND OF EFATE, VANUATU

'Going fishing again, huh?' queried a well-modulated foreign voice from somewhere just above and in front of my head. And I looked up from the newspaper I was reading before takeoff, into the smiling face of Alexander Losyukov, Russian Ambassador to Australia, on his way to present his credentials in Vanuatu and other parts.

He and his staff had been enormously helpful to me in my odyssey through Russia and eastern Europe earlier in the year (the subject of another book), so it was both fortuitous and pleasant to share an airline dinner together when I could debrief him about my Russian adventures as we flew from Sydney to Port Vila, the capital of Vanuatu. During the flight, Alexander let slip that he might have a few moments to spare during his visit and we briefly discussed the possibility of fishing together.

Billfish fly

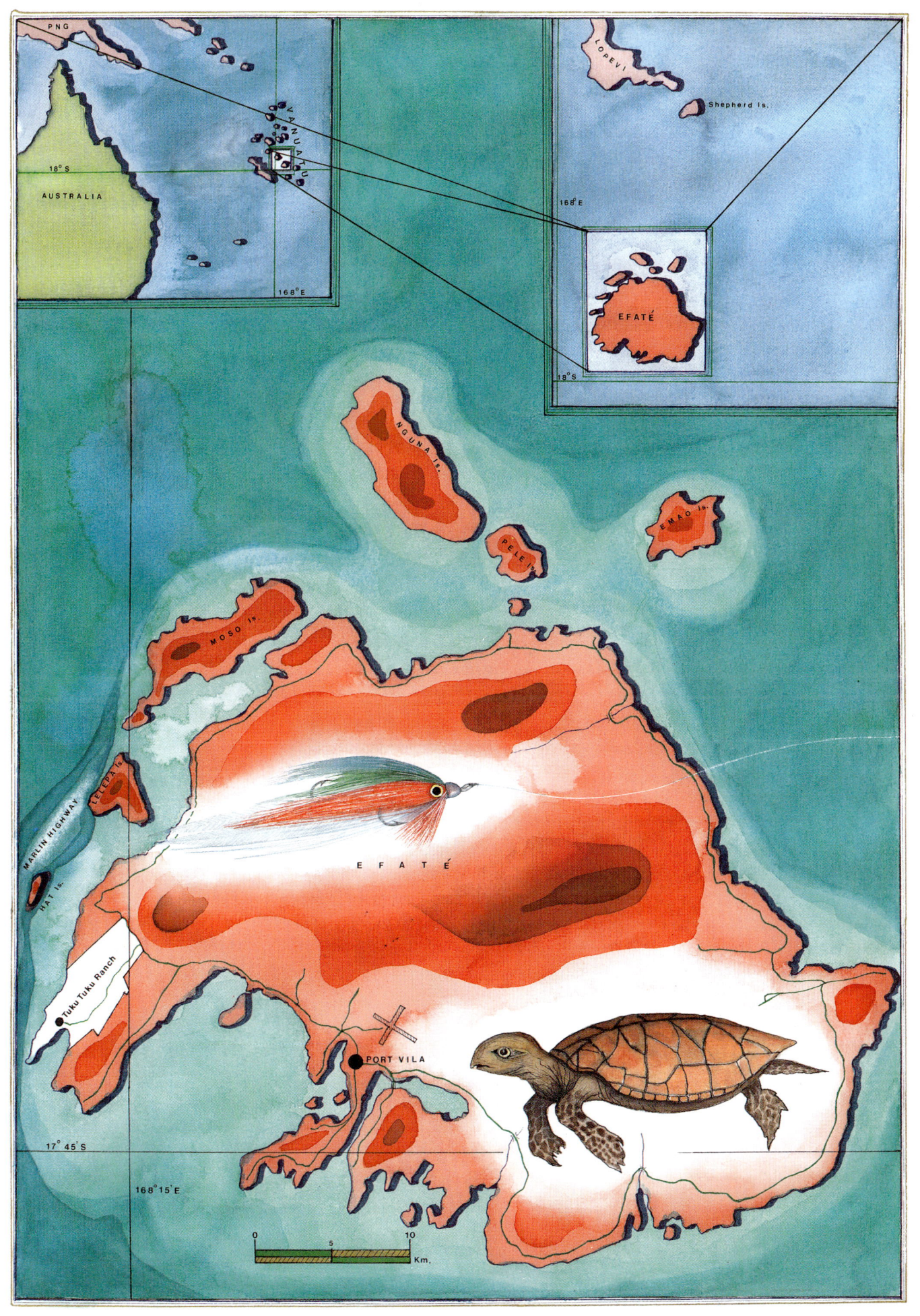

Mudmap of Efaté

Unfortunately he was too busy and it never came to pass, but I was left with Walter Mitty-esque fantasies of headlines announcing: 'Record fly-caught marlin taken in Vanuatu with Russian Ambassador acting as deckie!'

The name Vanuatu means 'Our Land', and the native Melanesian people—the *Ni-Vanuatu*—take pride in their million-year-old origins whose roots can be traced to southeast Asia, and so they established their land rights ages before European exploration. The first white man to step ashore in the islands was the Portuguese explorer de Quiros who, in 1606, believed the land to be part of the great southern continent. This theory was debunked in 1768 by the French explorer de Bougainville who established clearly that they were a small chain of islands.

Captain James Cook put the archipelago firmly on the map in 1774 with 46 days of cruising and survey, after which he named the group the New Hebrides. La Perouse followed in 1778, and in 1793 Captain Bligh, cast adrift from HMS *Bounty*, came upon the northern islands in the group during his involuntary island-hopping.

The next hundred years demonstrated colonialism at its worst. At first, the blatantly opportunistic export of sandalwood had the devastating effect of reducing a natural resource almost to extinction; at the same time the local island population was ravaged by new diseases introduced by the white arrivals. Then, in the 1860s, when the availability of sandalwood dried up, there evolved a shameful period when slave labour was exported to the sugar and cotton plantations of New Caledonia, Fiji, the Hawaiian Islands, Queensland and New South Wales.

In the latter part of the nineteenth century, Anglo-French rivalry for influence and control resulted, in 1906, in the extraordinary compromise known as the Condominium. Tagged 'the Pandemonium', the New Hebrides found themselves with two of everything, one French, and one English—schools, judicial systems, prisons, police, hospitals, churches and other absurdities. I remember visiting Port Vila in 1958 when alternate days were declared, one day French, the next English, changing at midnight. If my mind does not play me tricks, I seem to remember the French day was chaotic but more enjoyable. The madness continued for 74 years, including the Second World War when the islands were used as a vital advance base for allied troops in the Pacific. It ended in 1980 when, in spite of last ditch colonial stands by conservative planters—the so-called 'Coconut War'—the New Hebrides became the Republic of Vanuatu.

The 6000-acre cattle property, Tuku Tuku Ranch, lies twenty-five kilometres west of Port Vila on the Island of Efaté. This beautiful South Pacific haven was first developed in the late nineteenth century by a Frenchman and changed hands many times before it was finally purchased in the 1970s by the Trammel Crow family of Dallas, Texas. The Crows at one time also owned Vanuatu's largest hotel, the Intercontinental, as well as movie production companies in California and substantial American real estate holdings. In 1986, as the Crow

TUKU TUKU RANCH
- A Check-off List for the Travelling Fly-Fisherman

PRE-TRAVEL

Travellers from countries with established diplomatic relations with Vanuatu do not need visas. In all other cases visas can be obtained through the following address, where any queries may also be directed:
    Department of Foreign Affairs
    (Immigration)
    Private Mail Bag 051
    Port Vila
    Vanuatu
    Phone: INT.678.22913
    Fax: INT.678.23142.

CURRENCY

The Vanuatu VATU sells at approximately 80 to the $AUS and 105 to the $US. Australian and American currencies are readily negotiable in Vanuatu, and all major credit cards are accepted in Port Vila.

TRAVEL

Port Vila is an international airport with three return flights weekly from Sydney ($US600 return), two from Brisbane ($US500 return), and one from Melbourne ($US740 return). Flights are also available from New Zealand (Auckland) via New Caledonia; and for those approaching from the north and east Pacific, there are two return flights each week between Fiji (Nandi) and Port Vila. Costs can be markedly reduced in packages—the Tuku Tuku one-week/four-days fishing package is an example.

family's interests moved away from the South Pacific, Marcus Thomson, a young western hell-raiser from Iowa, responded to an advertisement and, after an interview, went to Vanuatu to inspect Tuku Tuku Ranch with a view to taking over management. On arrival, he found things in pretty bad shape but took on the challenge and, in 15 months (which included a devastating cyclone), he managed to clear and improve the place sufficiently to hammer out a suitable financial deal in which he attained a fifty-fifty partnership. A truly remarkable effort which has continued over the years, with Marcus gaining more equity as he rebuilt the Ranch into a viable cattle property supporting 2200 head of mixed beef cattle—meat for the local markets.

Marcus also added a homestead for his family (he married Vicki in 1991 and they have two daughters), good accommodation for his staff, guest accommodation, a turtle farm (to teach the locals to conserve the young turtles and only use the occasional big one for the pot), and a very effective day-visit program for the hotel trade in Port Vila, offering horse riding, snorkelling, sailing, beach barbecues, nature walks and other activities.

One of Marcus's great loves is fishing. From fly-fishing beginnings in the Rocky Mountains in America, he has become an active and experienced big-game fisherman and runs a range of charter packages at very attractive prices in his two boats, a Bertram 21 and a Blackwatch 34. Vanuatu is well known for its big-game fishery, the most productive action taking place out of Port Vila, to the south and west around the island where conditions on the 'Marlin Highway' can be lumpy at times. The Waterfront Bar and Grill in Port Vila, home of the game-fishing club and adjacent to the boat moorings, is the 'Hemingway-Havana' of Vanuatu; not as big as the waterfront at Cairns maybe, but equally colourful. Most charters operate from this point, close to the hotels, but Marcus, with his own harbour and guest accommodation at Tuku Tuku, can put clients on the Marlin Highway in a very short time (even for those opting to stay in town).

Husband, father, fisherman, bushman, rancher, engineer, cattleman, horseman, turtle-farmer, community-group leader, workaholic and loved by his family and staff, Marcus Thomson may not be the 'last of the Mohicans' in Vanuatu, but he's 'awful close to it'. In his book *Conversations with Cannibals*, which focuses on those individuals who personify the spirit of the old South Pacific, Michael Krieger devotes a whole chapter to Marcus entitled 'Ramrod' because of Thomson's hardworking honesty. In the closing lines, when Krieger is talking to Marcus about local political pull, the conversation goes like this:

(Marcus): *I'm honest with people, and I don't care how bad it hurts, I tell the truth. If it's the President of this country or if it's the President of the USA, if I don't like his attitude, I'll say something.*

(Krieger): *Well, that might be a quick way to get thrown out of here.*

(Marcus): *Yeah, that's right, but you can't surrender your integrity. You have to keep some of your pride, and if my straight honesty and position isn't good enough for 'em, then I don't wanta be here.*

ACCOMMODATION

Tuku Tuku Ranch offers the following attractive packages:

a. Bunkhouse accommodation including transfers, all meals and access to property activities (except game fishing) at $US100 per person/night.
b. Campsite-site accommodation on application.
c. A week's fishing package: Wednesday to Wednesday, including return airfare from Brisbane, transfers, bunkhouse accommodation, all meals, access to property activities, one return trip to Port Vila during the week AND four days' game fishing at $US1650 per person (minimum four anglers).
d. Other purpose-designed packages (to include non-anglers for example) on application.

Tuku Tuku Ranch address is:
Thomsons Expeditions
Box 333
Port Vila
Vanuatu.
Phone: INT.678.23096
Fax: INT.678.27215

Hotel accommodation in Port Vila is available from around $US140 per night when transfers to the Ranch should be negotiated with Tuku Tuku.

BOAT CHARTER

Outside the packages, Tuku Tuku game-boat charters are available at the following prices (for the boat/day):
Bertram 21: $US350 (maximum 3 anglers)
Blackwatch 34: $US700 (maximum 6 anglers)

FACILITIES

Port Vila is a major town with full shopping, banking, restaurant, motel, travel and medical facilities. It is approximately 40 minutes from Tuku Tuku Ranch and taxi fares are approximately $US20 one way.

Barbecue Beach with Hat Island and the 'Highway' in the background

Tuku Tuku snorkelling hole

If Dean Butler is the Indiana Jones of the North, then Marcus Thomson must be the John Wayne of the South Pacific.

Getting to Efaté and Tuku Tuku Ranch

Port Vila is an international airport with three return flights from Sydney, two from Brisbane and one from Melbourne each week. For those approaching direct from the eastern Pacific, return flights operate twice weekly from Nandi in Fiji to Port Vila.

On arrival in Port Vila, Tuku Tuku Ranch transport meets customers at the airport for the 40-minute drive to the ranch (or ten minutes to town) and will make the return trip at the end of the stay.

Accommodation

Marcus has built a very comfortable, modern, tropical 16-bed bunkhouse near the homestead. It has its own bathroom complex, sweeping verandah, barbecue pit and 240-volt power supply. It is ideal for a party of anglers for whom a very attractive package is offered which includes all meals and access to property facilities (the only extras being game boat charter, alcohol and personal items). Sometime in the future he plans to build smaller, self-contained guest cabins at Tuku Tuku. The use of beachside camp sites can be negotiated.

Alternatively, guests can stay in Port Vila and Marcus will arrange transport to and from the Ranch for fishing. Hotels from one- to five-star quality are available at varying prices.

The Waters

Billfish are the primary sportfish in Vanuatu, and the Marlin Highway, just out from Tuku Tuku, is as good a place as any to chase them. For the angler staying at the Ranch, the Highway has the added advantage of quick access early in the morning and is only minutes from a shower at the end of the fishing day. FADs are anchored at the southern end of the Highway and also south of Port Vila.

For the fly-fisherman more interested in smaller game, trevally, bonito, barracuda, queenfish, wahoo, mackerel and other pelagics are plentiful around the reefs and drop-offs, and may be cast to from the shore as well.

As yet, recreational fishing needs no licence in Vanuatu. Marcus practises all conservation measures in his boats.

LEFT
Marcus and his coxswain in the Bertram

RIGHT
The waterfront at Port Vila

Tackle, Flies and Fishing Matters

The fly-fisherman wishing to chase billfish in Vanuatu should refer to the previous chapter. When I was in Vanuatu, both Marcus and I chased marlin on the fly for the first time for both of us. Nonetheless, in two days fishing, we enticed one 200-pound fish, via three teasers (handled by Marcus alone), to a smaller version of the fly painted in watercolour in this chapter, only to observe a very exciting last-minute refusal. Marcus is keen to pursue fly-fishing, the Highway is a magnificent stretch for billfish, and knowing Marcus's enthusiasm, he will have the fly routine worked out and practised by the time this book goes to print.

For the fly-fisherman who chooses to go after lesser quarry, I would suggest a good ten-weight outfit with a top-quality, super-smooth reel, 200 yards of backing and a leader of 30-pound monofilament (or 20-pound if records are sought), twisted to a loop to the fly line and including a heavier shock tippet. Sauris, Goose Creeks, and Blue and White Deceivers are probably the best flies, although the Chartreuse Deceiver often does wonders in the tropics.

The November 1995 Visit

I left the Russian Ambassador at the luggage collection conveyor at Vila airport at 9 pm on Wednesday 1 November to meet Alfred Vanva, the Tuku Tuku Ranch foreman. After loading my gear into the back of a twin-cab pick-up, joined by Alfred and his family, I left for the Ranch where we were met by Vicki Thomson at the bunkhouse 40 minutes later. Marcus was absent in Fiji and would return the following evening, so Vicki arranged a visit to town the next morning, followed by a tour of the ranch in the afternoon. Then, when Marcus returned, we would discuss tactics before fishing all day Friday and Saturday. I was due to return to Sydney on Sunday lunchtime. . .all too soon.

Not surprisingly, I found that Port Vila had grown considerably in my 37-year absence. I found a bustling town with attractive shops and roadside stalls, and a wide range of eateries aimed at the tourist trade. Many banks are represented, the waterfront is colourful and exciting, there are a number of luxury hotels, and the visiting angler will find much to his liking, although the fly-fisherman should bring his own tackle. The unit of currency, the Vanuatu Vatu, sold at that time at around 80 to the Australian dollar and 105 to the American. Both overseas currencies are readily accepted in town, as are all major credit cards.

Back at Tuku Tuku in the afternoon, Alfred guided me around the Ranch. We looked at the stock, pastures, fencing and building improvements and I was left in awe of the progress that had been made. We examined the turtle farm, Alfred's pet coconut crab (huge), the pigs and the horses and found them in fine fettle. I was apprised of Marcus' plans for the bay and future wharves, we looked at the snorkelling hole, the beach barbecue facility, the turquoise water and white sand, and I began to understand the Thomsons' enthusiasm. Finally I met some more of the locals and gained a better idea of why the entire project works so well.

TIME ZONE

The time zone throughout Vanuatu is eleven hours ahead of Greenwich Mean Time and remains so throughout the year.

ELECTRICITY

The town supply is 240 volt AC. Generated 240 volt AC is available at Tuku Tuku Ranch between 6 am and 11 pm.

CLIMATE AND CLOTHING

Vanuatu is temperate tropical with temperatures ranging from the low 20s to the low 30s Celsius. The wet season runs from December through March when the humidity can be high. Light casual clothing is best at all times; sneakers are suitable for most activities but appropriate extra footwear should be considered for walking, riding, and rock fishing. A hat, sunscreen and insect repellent are essential. AND CHECK WITH YOUR DOCTOR WELL AHEAD OF YOUR ADVENTURE: Vanuatu is a malaria area.

TACKLE AND FISHING

The billfish season runs from late October through April. For billfish fly-fishing tackle requirements refer to the previous chapter; Marcus holds a full range of tackle for the conventional fisherman. For pelagic fly-fishing, ten-weight outfits are ideal. Good quality, smooth-drag reels capable of holding at least 200 yards of backing are essential, and the angler should carry 20- and 30-pound monofilament and some shock-tippet material. Sauris (2/0 to 4/0), Goose Creeks (2/0), and White, Blue and Chartreuse Deceivers (2/0) are the best flies.

Marcus returned that evening and, together with Alfred, we worked out a strategy for the next two days. We would patrol the Highway in the Bertram (the Blackwatch was expected in January 1996), using three hookless lures astern at varying distances. Alfred would drive, Marcus would work the teasers from the starboard quarter, and I would stand by in the port quarter with most of my fly line stripped into a bucket ready to cast. With differences only in the number of teaser operators, the use of hookless lures rather than live teasers, and the size of my fly (too small?), this forecast the procedure to which I was later introduced in New Guinea.

We started at dawn on Friday 3 November and patrolled all day without a sighting. Marcus was disappointed; in the previous week he had been involved with three or four marlin daily, but now, despite considerable seabird activity above baitfish shoals—ideal conditions— there wasn't a single riser. I didn't realise at the time that I was on the first rung of the learning ladder.

The following afternoon in perfect weather with increased baitfish activity, the gamefish drought continued. I knew Marcus was keen for me to have a go at a marlin but I wasn't sure whether he would put up with another fruitless day flogging the Highway. So, reluctantly, I suggested that, maybe, we should have a go at the pelagics around the reefs for a change.

Oh ye of little faith! He made it abundantly clear that I came to Tuku Tuku to go for a billfish on the fly and he would do all in his power to make it happen! It was an important lesson about the use of time-on-the-water in the marlin-odds equation.

A few minutes later, as Marcus was head-down attending to some other tackle, I saw a double splash around the outer teaser...then a dorsal fin...then a sickle tail. 'Marcus', I stammered, 'We've got company!' Everything started to happen at once. Marcus jumped to retrieve the outer teaser and the fish disappeared, only to come back hard at the second. This was pulled in and the fish pounced on the third. By now, with only one man on the teasers, there was a certain amount of junk hanging over the transom as Marcus, working like a legless hopscotch player, recovered the final lure.

With about 40 feet to go and the marlin clearly lit up and visible, I yelled for the cut. Alfred disengaged the motor, Marcus whipped the third teaser and I cast the fly, short because I was unprepared for the weight in the strong breeze. Nonetheless, the marlin went for it, 30 feet astern and close to his bill. I think it was probably the most exciting moment I can remember in my last 20 years of fly-fishing. In the event, at that *moment critiqué*, the marlin either saw the transom, the two astonishingly excited faces peering at him and the mess of recovered teasers, or he didn't like the fly—perhaps all of those things. Because, just short of the fly, he turned and swam effortlessly away, not to be seen again. Maybe it was all pre-ordained, because (as I discovered later in New Guinea) had I hooked him, my leader rig would have been hard pushed to last the distance.

We motored slowly back to harbour, making plans and discussing tactics for the future, talking about fishing packages involving the Blackwatch. I hadn't hooked a fish in the two short days' fishing I had given myself at Vanuatu, but the visit was my most exciting so far in the Southwest Pacific. That evening we talked further about Marcus's plans and fishing packages; some very attractive options are given in the check-off list.

I was very sorry to leave the next day. I felt I had only just begun to play at a very exciting sport and badly wanted to stay on with Marcus and keep at it: an indication of the intoxication and addictiveness of the game. But it was not to be; I had commitments elsewhere.

Incidentally, each day when we were out on the Highway, Vicki made us the most delicious chilli-tuna sandwiches for lunch. She tells me the filling can also be used as a dip; this is her recipe:

Vicki Thomson's Chilli-Tuna Mix

2 kg skipjack tuna meat (cooked with butter in foil, cooled and broken into small pieces)
Chopped fresh chilli (to taste)
6 hard-boiled eggs (chopped)
¼ cup onions (chopped)
½ cup dill pickle (chopped)
½ cup dill pickle juice
½ cup mayonnaise
Salt and pepper (to taste)

MIX the tuna, chilli, egg, onion and pickle in a large mixing bowl and season with salt and pepper. Add the pickle juice and mayonnaise slowly while trying to achieve the desired thickness.
REFRIGERATE for two hours, then serve as a dip with taco chips, or as a sandwich filling with a squeeze of lemon.

10
OFF MADANG IN PAPUA NEW GUINEA

I ONCE BROKE my shoulder in New Guinea, water-skiing near Port Moresby after an excellent lunch. That was a long time ago in the 1960s, when I was in the Navy and enjoyed regular visits to that colourful country to top up the Oil Fuel Installation on Manus Island in the Bismarck Archipelago.

Nearly thirty years after my last visit (with independence being granted in 1975), press headlines gloomed stories about rampant and violent crime, high-level administrative corruption, squandered natural resources, urban services interruptions, lack of health care, illiteracy, devalued currency and climbing inflation with a steadily declining GDP. What's more, I have friends who had, over the years, quit the country to escape these problems. So, although I was greatly looking forward to some saltwater fly-fishing in the Bismarck Sea, I wasn't so enthusiastic about the prospects of travelling through Port Moresby and jumping the Highlands to get there.

LEFT
The author into his first marlin (conventional gear) . . . (DEAN BUTLER)

RIGHT
. . . which is tagged prior to release

As it transpired, my travels gave me but a one-hour changeover each way between flights at Port Moresby and even less in the Highlands at Goroka. The Moresby terminal was hot, unattractive and dirty, but hardly intimidating; the Highlands were cool, attractive and comfortable: short-term first impressions of little depth or consequence. A few days before I passed through, a popular restaurant in Port Moresby had been held up (not uncommon) by a local gang known as *rascols*, but a diner had managed to find his pistol while reaching inside his coat for his wallet, and shoot four of the crooks (uncommon; and one wonders if he attracted additional frequent-flyer points when he paid for his interrupted tucker by plastic card?). And in Madang on the way home, flight schedules were in chaos due to rain and when we were eventually called to board the aircraft I saw my luggage being loaded into another aeroplane! It was saved with only minutes to spare.

Out fishing, and in the evening when we returned, the conversation would sometimes drift from talk about currents, flies, tackle and billfish, to corruption and the squandering of natural resources. Mention was made of international companies who, after denuding the timber in their own backyards, were moving, with ministerial assent, into New Guinea where the forests were being sold off at knockdown prices to attract short-term investment and liquidity. New Guinea timber was disappearing and erosion was on the increase; indeed, I had never seen the waters through which I used to navigate so dirty. Erosion? I had insufficient time to find out. Then back to fish and the discussion might turn from the selling-off of commercial fishing franchises for the same short-term economic reasons to international fishing concerns operating with purse-seine nets, vacuuming the oceans to extinction for quick profit.

Whatever the causes, the waters around Madang were discoloured with grit, the currents weak and the game-fish activity slow—while I was there anyway. Admittedly, the northwest monsoon was yet to blow in for the anglers who were awaiting it so eagerly. But, with a few praiseworthy exceptions in isolated areas, there was a pervading sense of 'exploit now because it may not be there tomorrow'. . .an epitaph to post-colonial decay in the southwest Pacific.

All doom and gloom? Certainly not. The words which follow are written to portray northern New Guinea and Dean Butler's Sportfishing Adventures as one of the truly great game fly-fishing arenas in this world; and that's exactly what it is. It would be mischievous, however, not to point out the pitfalls to the travelling angler before switching to the superlative. Fishermen should remember that Dean's experienced organisation will guide them through unscathed, transfers at Moresby and Madang included. After that it's all downhill and exciting laid-back bliss.

'Indiana' Butler has fly-fished in Papua New Guinea for over 15 years. In the beginning he chased black and spot-tail bass from river camp sites then, in 1987, he started a guiding and tuition service, using aluminium dinghies by day returning to a chartered mothership in the evening. Four years later he joined Brett Middleton of Dylup Plantation

MADANG
- A Check-off List for the Travelling Fly-Fisherman

PRE-TRAVEL

Visas are required for all but some South Pacific Island Nations. Papua New Guinea diplomatic or consular offices should be contacted for details.

CURRENCY

The $US will buy 1.27 Papua New Guinea Kina; the $AUS will buy 0.95 Kina. American and Australian currency is negotiable in New Guinea. For those using one of Dean Butler's pre-paid packages, they will only need sufficient cash for alcohol, departure tax, duty-free items and items of a personal nature (say $US300).

TRAVEL

Port Moresby is an international airport with connections to Australia, Singapore and Hong Kong. The Australian return flights operate from Sydney through Brisbane three times each week with same-day Madang connections. Return fares to Madang are $US900 ex-Sydney and $US800 ex-Brisbane. Dean Butler's Sportfishing Adventures can arrange these ex-package requirements at reduced cost.

north of Madang when Brett acquired the Steber 36 *Talio*. With decades of combined fishing experience between them, they established an operation in which Dean handles the marketing from his Queensland office and instruction afloat, and Brett provides the boat, crew, accommodation and meals from his Dylup Plantation.

The Middletons, going back to Brett's grandfather, have run coconut and cocoa plantations in the Madang area since the 1920s. Kulili Plantation on Karkar Island is the original family home and dates back to Lutheran missionary times in the 1890s. It was next owned by 'Karkar' Schmitt, a German, from whom the property was expropriated following the Treaty of Versailles after the Great War. Today the home of the second Middleton generation, Brett's father and mother, it is a very beautiful and fascinating place. Steeped in history, including Japanese occupation during the Second World War, it is the quintessence of the old South Pacific. A large rambling house constructed with heavy wooden beams and polished floors, it overlooks the sea through tropical gardens and coconut palms. Big overhead fans move the air as the trade winds breathe through louvred windows; a smiling staff keeps things shipshape, and one rather expects to bump into Somerset Maugham in a pith helmet, offering gin and tonics when the sun passes the yardarm.

In contrast, Brett's mainland plantation, Dylup, which he took over from a public company in 1988, has a more modern homestead and includes air-conditioned directors' quarters, a swimming pool, an outdoor bar and eating area. The Butler/Middleton fishing packages make use of both plantations, with clients enjoying some time in the directors' quarters at Dylup and some on Karkar Island where they are normally housed in bungalows at Wadau (Brett's brother, Derrick's property), or in guest houses on Kulili Plantation.

The range of packages offered includes a week of new-frontier game fishing in luxury around Karkar Island, a trip to Arrjim Island on the remote south coast of west New Britain to fish for bass, or dedicated week-long workshops to learn big-game fly-fishing from basics. Some of these activities can be combined, or packages can be tailored to meet most individual requirements. Prices are quoted ex-Madang, normally for four anglers, although non-anglers are welcome at much reduced rates, depending on available accommodation. In addition, Dean markets other packages, not associated with New Guinea, for game and pelagic fishing across the top of Australia from the Gold Coast to the Kimberley. A week of fly-fishing off Madang with this organisation—or, better still, a workshop—would, in my opinion, be the best classroom in the Southern Hemisphere in which to learn big-game fly-fishing.

Getting to Madang

Port Moresby is an international airport with direct flights connecting Hong Kong, Singapore and Australia. The Australian flights operate three times each week and connect with Madang the same day. Once in Madang, Brett Middleton arranges transfers to and from Dylup Plantation (about 45 minutes each way).

PACKAGES

The Bismarck Sea fishing package includes four nights at Dylup, three at Kulili, transfers ex-Madang, all meals and twin-share accommodation, six full days fishing in *Talio* with all tackle (except fly tackle), full laundry service at Dylup, and guiding and tuition. Costs for a party of four are $US1800 per head ex-Madang. Special packages, visits to Arrjim Island bass fishing camp, and reductions for non-anglers can be arranged with Dean Butler. The workshop package includes transfers ex-Mandang, six nights at Dylup, two at Kulili, all meals and twin-share accommodation, five full days fishing in *Talio* (providing own fly-fishing tackle), full laundry service at Dylup, and guiding and tuition. Anglers will spend a day preparing tackle and knots, five days on the water with maximum emphasis on improving individual skills, and a final day of analysis of techniques. The cost per person ex-Madang is $US2175. Flights in and out of Madang, alcohol, visa fees, departure tax, travel insurance, duty-free items and items of a personal nature are not included in the packages. All details can be obtained through:

Dean Butler's Sportfishing Adventures
PO Box 55
Edge Hill
Queensland 4870
Australia
Phone: INT.61.(0)70.532940
(From November 1997:
61.(0)7.40532940)
Fax: INT.61.(0)70.531009
(From November 1997:
61.(0)7.40531009)
Mobile: INT.61.015249818

Accommodation

The air-conditioned directors' quarters at Dylup Plantation has two bedrooms, both with en-suite bathrooms; one has a double and a single bed, the other has three singles. A comfortable lounge room with fridge and coffee-making facilities (and a photographic gallery of big fish) separates the two bedrooms. Immediately outside, a swimming pool set in lush tropical gardens leads to an undercover bar and eating area. The plantation has its own small zoo of colourful birds and animals.

On Karkar Island, the two beach bungalows at Wadau can accommodate up to six people and have separate bathrooms and overhead fans. The guest houses at Kulili can look after similar numbers in similar style and, in both cases, meals are taken in the adjacent homesteads, although lunch is normally eaten afloat.

The Waters

The Bismarck Sea is rich in some of the world's most sought-after game fish. Marlin, sailfish, tuna and others congregate to feed on the baitfish supply carried by the warm south sea currents flowing through Vitiaz Strait and around the volcanic islands off Madang, sometimes within 100 yards of the shore. Pelagics are in abundance off the reefs, and bass, the strongest fresh-water fish in the world, are plentiful in New Britain rivers and elsewhere.

Tackle, Flies and Fishing Matters

The fly-fisherman needs to bring his own tackle to Madang. Although the packages include the provision of conventional tackle, fly-fishing gear is not provided. The fly-fisherman wishing to chase billfish off Madang should refer to Chapter 8 concerning tackle.

For those pursuing lesser quarry, for sport or for baitfish for teasers, the ten-weight outfit described in the previous chapter is also suitable around Madang, where I found the Chartreuse Deceiver the most successful fly, although other Deceivers were also very useful.

The November 1995 Visit

The flight to Port Moresby left Sydney at nine o'clock in the morning on Wednesday 8 November, there was one stop at Brisbane and we landed in Papua New Guinea in stifling heat five hours later. Peter Pakula, the internationally-known lure maker from Runaway Bay in Queensland, boarded the flight in Brisbane; we were to share a planned week together fishing with Dean and Brett out of Madang.

The flight to Madang via Goroka was uneventful and the Highlands pleasantly cool. Brett met us at the airport, and with Dean, drove us to Plantation House at Dylup—a very comfortable haven after a long day, many kilometres and a wide range of temperatures. During dinner beside the swimming pool, we discussed plans for the next few days. The talk then drifted naturally to the recent spate of discoloured water, weak currents and little game fish activity. Even though the previous week

Mudmap of the Bismarck Sea off Madang

had been a disappointment, it was planned, in the next two days, to examine the area out to Karkar Island and beyond to see what would turn up.

A group of observers from a Sydney radio sports show and travel organisations joined us on board *Talio* the next day to get a feel for this new and exotic game-fishing playground. The water was 'green' and full of grit, the currents insufficient to shift the grit and clean it, and the bird life and baitfish activity minimal. So we trolled conventional rigs with hooked lures (seven of them) between Karkar Island and the coast, hoping to induce a strike.

Mid-afternoon, the breeze died, the sea became calm and things began to look decidedly more 'fishy'. I had kindly been given first strike but wasn't feeling very optimistic, then the port side outer lure was struck by a marlin. He spat the hook but came a second time and hooked up solidly. The fight, on 130-pound tackle, took only five or ten minutes before the fish, estimated at around 180 pounds, was tagged, photographed and released. He was my first marlin and, therefore I guess, a milestone. But I was left with two conflicting thoughts: catching that size fish on heavy conventional gear gave me practically no thrill at all and I had my doubts about bigger marlin, although I'm prepared to be persuaded otherwise; on the other hand, I thought, how in hell do you control one of those monsters on a fly rod? Surely *that* would be a monumental high.

On Friday 10 November we were up at dawn to troll conventional gear south around Karkar Island, past Bagabag Island and northeast to a volcanic seamount, still trying to induce a strike in what is normally a great billfish area. But once again most of the day's effort was fruitless. I hasten to add that if we had gone to the reefs and drop-offs with ten-weights, small flies and poppers, we could have had a heap of fun with the pelagics. But we sought bigger game.

During this lull Dean examined my gear from spool to fly. That is when we found some connection deficiencies and, from that time forward, I used the rig detailed in Chapter 8.

In the early afternoon Dean persuaded Brett to recover the lures and put out teasers; it looked like a no-action day, and there was that factor of time-on-the-water to consider. By late afternoon, with a dot score, we reeled in and headed for home. Then, on rounding Karkar Island towards dusk, we saw frantic seabird and baitfish activity and raced to the spot with time only to stream a couple of conventional lures (. . .time-on-the-water again?). Within 15 minutes, Peter Pakula had another 180-pound marlin alongside for tagging, photos and release. Including Vanuatu, that meant three ideal (fly) size marlin in four days on the water. One had come to the fly, and two had been taken conventionally. Would those two have come to the fly? What would have been the outcome? It can be addictive, this type of fishing; it can also be expressed in terms of hours and hours of boredom interspersed by short moments of staggering exhilaration.

We went to Kulili Plantation on Karkar Island the next morning, and I met Brett's father and mother, John and Anna Middleton. After lunch, while the others went fishing again in *Talio*, I stayed behind in one of the guest houses, writing my notes and making sketches. As I worked I kept imagining Ensign Nellie Forbush jumping out of the jungle singing: 'I'm gonna wash that man right outta my hair!' Kulili *really is* the old South Pacific.

FACILITIES

Madang has a reasonable range of hotel/motel/restaurants, shops, banks, garages and full health services. There is also a small hospital and a doctor on Karkar Island.

TIME ZONE

Papua New Guinea is ten hours ahead of Greenwich Mean Time and remains so throughout the year.

ELECTRICITY

Dylup and Kulili operate on generated 240 volt AC supply.

The fishermen had little success fishing, but in the evening, on the lawns in front of the house with the beach at our feet, we ate barbecued lamb and chocolate mousse washed down with chilled Wolff Blass claret while a full moon rose through the coconut palms, silhouetting the trunks against the reflected light on the ocean. Sigh you sinners, sigh!

After one night in the guest house at Kulili, we left in *Talio* early the next morning to spend two days at sea. The plan was to continue the billfish hunt as progress was made towards Hankow Reef, then to catch live teaser bait and try for dogtooth tuna, and afterwards to anchor on the reef (or at Crown Island) overnight and continue the chase early the next day. But once again the billfish didn't show up, and so to Hankow Reef to take a number of rainbow runners for bait.

Under the IGFA record listings for fly-caught fish, all line classes in the dogtooth tuna column have remained vacant since recording began. Considering the depth at which these fish operate, that is not surprising. During several months of experimenting, however, Dean had designed a teaser which would bring these fish to the surface to a position where they could be cast to with a fly. In fact, he and his friends had hooked big tuna before, but none had been landed. His teaser rod is custom-built, coarse-graphite about eight feet long with a small baitcaster reel, and the monofilament passes from the reel, into the centre of the rod and out the tip (to prevent tangles when the teaser is jerked clear to allow substitution with the fly). A live, swimming rainbow runner is attached to the end of the monofilament and streamed through the starboard outrigger pole (assuming a right-handed fly caster) and manned at short stay. The fly caster operates from the port quarter with line stripped into a bucket, ready to cast. All eyes from transom to tuna tower watch the teaser and, when the doggy appears from down under, on a single command the motor is disengaged to conform with the record rules, the teaser is whipped away from the fish and the fly substituted in a few short seconds of shouting and orchestrated chaos.

One fly-caught tuna was boated that afternoon, a small fish as tuna go and not a record claim because the engine was engaged at hookup. But he provided the basis for a delicious numus (pickled fish; see the recipe in Chapter 4) that evening, and there is no doubt about it: once one has developed a taste for sweet raw fish—soused, pickled, *gravdlaxed* or plain—one thinks twice about ever again eating plain old fish and chips.

We anchored that night off Crown Island, a good choice because the wind increased overnight and a fair chop was running when we returned to Hankow Reef early on the morning of Monday 13 November. All was quiet for the first couple of hours, then at twelve minutes past ten, Brett yelled from the bridge: 'Doggy! Doggy! Doggy!' The fish chomped on the teaser before it could be whipped clear, but let it go to come a second time. This time the teaser was pulled high, Brett disengaged the clutch and Dean cast. The fly sank. I lost sight of it and the fish but Dean held them both. The tuna switched his attention

CLIMATE AND CLOTHING:

At latitude five degrees south, the Bismarck Sea area is hot and humid (I mean Aitch-Oh-Tee!). The more humid season runs from November through April during the Northwest Monsoon, but the heat out fishing is always such that designer fishing shirts with lots of labels and useless pockets act like clingwrap, trapping in pints of perspiration. Ordinary cotton T-shirts or singlets are far more comfortable. Dress in the evening is casual, a clean shirt and slacks (or shorts) after a shower is all that's needed, and remember there is a full laundry service at Dylup. While most prefer to go bare-footed at sea, a pair of sneakers is sufficient on shore. A hat, good dark glasses and sunscreen are essential. AND CHECK WITH YOUR DOCTOR WELL AHEAD OF YOUR ADVENTURE: Papua New Guinea is a malaria area. Despite taking all advertised precautions and preventative drugs, I contracted malaria four months after my return to Australia from New Guinea.

TACKLE AND FISHING

The billfish season runs from November through April. For billfish fly-fishing tackle, refer to Chapter 8. For pelagic fly-fishing, ten-weights are ideal. Good quality, smooth-drag reels capable of holding at least 200 yards of backing are essential, and the angler should carry 20- and 30-pound monofilament and some shock-tippet material. Sauris (2/0 to 4/0), Goose Creeks (2/0) and other Deceivers are the best flies with the Chartreuse Deceiver being exceptional.
Licences are not required for recreational fishing in New Guinea.

to the fly, Dean hooked up and leant backwards as line and backing disappeared. Brett engaged the clutch to clear the reef, and the tuna, as expected, bored for the bottom.

Twenty-four and a half minutes later, after strenuous pumping (fascinating to watch on a U-bent fly rod), the gaff went in, the doggy was boated, the photographs taken and the cold beer opened. It wasn't a big fish—26½ pounds on 22-pound test—there are much bigger ones around, but it proved it was possible to boat a dogtooth tuna on the fly. It was weighed that evening on a certified scale at Karkar Island, Dean and Brett completed the IGFA record form and Peter and I acted as witnesses.

On Tuesday 14 November, after a free morning when I worked on my notes and sketches, we said our farewells to Kulili and returned to Dylup in a tropical downpour. Wednesday 15 was the final fishing day, and although we flogged the water from Cape Croisilles to Bagabag Island and sighted two marlin, we had no follows and no successes. The next day I flew south, luckily sidestepping luggage problems in Madang, as mentioned, and fortunately coinciding with Qantas's 75th birthday (I was made aware of this as I flew from Port Moresby to Sydney and was offered chocolate birthday cake and champagne).

By now, the reader may be thinking that billfish around Madang and Vanuatu are few and far between. Let me hasten to point out that past and recent catch records indicate much greater profileration, particularly of sailfish around Madang. The prime season is from November to April, with the start dependent to some extent on the arrival of the northwest monsoon. I shall return for another go because I believe these are truly great fisheries, because of the hospitatlity, comfort and scenery, and because I have had my first 'fix' of the excitement of big-game fly-fishing and found it totally addictive.

I mentioned raw fish and how much I enjoy it. Well, at Kulili Plantation, Brett's mother, Anna, served 'Marlin *Gravdlax*' one evening—perhaps it should be called 'Gravdmarlin'—and it was nothing short of sensational. Here is her recipe:

Anna's Gravdmarlin

2 part-fillets (45 cm long) blue marlin (skin on)
2 cups rock salt
2 cups brown sugar
1 tbsp white pepper (crushed)
½ cup fresh dill
1 tsp turmeric
Vegetable oil

MIX the spices together and rub into the fish. Place the first fillet skinside down and the other skinside up on top of the first, cover with the remaining spices and wrap in foil. Cover with a board and press with a heavy weight in the fridge for 24 hours. Pour off the collected brine, lay both pieces skin-side down, cover with oil and leave in the fridge for three days.

REMOVE, wash off the brine and the oil, and carve into thin servings.

Sauce
4 tsp Dijon mustard
1 tsp powdered English mustard
3 tsp sugar
2 tsp vinegar
⅓ cup olive oil
4 tspn fresh dill

MIX the vinegar and spices together and beat in the oil.

(Trivial note: *'First catch your Marlin!'*)

Fascinating to watch on a U-bent fly rod . . . but necessary for Dean Butler to achieve this world-record dogtooth tuna

Index

Aborigine (al), 36–38, 41
Air New Zealand, 12
Albury, Australia, 21, 22
Alexandra, New Zealand, 13
Alpine Angler, The, 6, 32, 33
Alpine National Park, Australia, 19–21, 34
Ansett International, 6
Archerfish, 41, 44, 50
Arttech Warehouse, 6
Auckland, New Zealand, 12
Australia 20, 24, 31, 33, 36–38, 56–58, 60, 64, 65, 69, 71, 88
Australian Museum, Sydney, 28, 29
Australian Resorts, 29, 35

Backing, gel-spun, 74, 75
Bagabag Island, New Guinea, 29, 94
Bamaga, Australia, 64, 65, 68, 71
Barracuda, 29, 38, 57, 5g, 61, 62, 65, 83
Barramundi, 35, 38, 40, 41, 43–45, 47, 49, 50, 52, 53, 64, 65, 68–71
Beech, Chris (Striker Flies), 33, 40, 70
Benalla, Australia, 70, 71
Bethune,
    Greg, 6, 64, 65, 68, 69, 71
    Jennifer, 6, 64, 71
    Joseph, 64, 65
Big Game, 72, 75
Billfish, 38, 57, 59, 64, 72, 73, 76, 83–85, 92–94
Bismarck (Sea and Archipelago), 87, 89, 90
Bonefish, 57, 59–62
Bonito, 71, 83
Bream, 49, 50, 59, 61, 65
Brisbane, Australia, 28, 31, 64, 67, 80–82, 88, 90
Bromley, Ross, 6, 21, 24, 25
Brumby Base, El Questro, 47–49
Burrell,
    Will, 6, 45, 48, 52, 53
    Celia, 6, 45, 48, 53
Butler, Dean, 6, 49, 72, 82, 88–90, 92–94

Cairns, Australia, 28, 31, 33, 35, 40, 64, 65, 67, 68, 81
Cambridge Gulf, Australia, 49, 50
Canberra, Australia, 8, 24, 26, 33, 62
Cape Don, Australia, 36–39

Capricorn Mist 64, 65, 67, 68, 70, 71
Carp, European, 20, 25
Carpentaria, Gulf of, 6, 63–66, 69
Carpentaria Seafaris, 64, 65, 68, 71
Chamberlain River (and Gorge), El Questro, 45, 50, 52 53
Christchurch, New Zealand, 12
Christmas, Island, Indian Ocean, 58, 62
Clayton, John 6, 17
Clunies(-) Ross, 56, 57, 60
Cobia, 65, 68
Cobourg Peninsula, Australia, 36–41
Cocos (Keeling) Islands, 6, 53–62
Cocos (Islands in the Group),
    Home, 56–58, 60, 61
    West, 56–61
    South, 56, 61
    Horsburgh, 56
    Direction, 56
    Keeling, 56
Crocodile(s), 33, 41, 48–50, 52, 69
Conservation, 11, 35, 49, 83
Cotterell River, Australia, 64, 70
Craigs Hut, Australia, 19, 20, 22, 25
Crystal Creek, Australia, 64

Dandongadale River, Australia, 21, 25
Dansey Pass, New Zealand, 13, 17
Dartmouth Dam, Australia, 22, 24
Darwin, Australia, 37, 40, 45, 49, 52, 53, 56, 60
Doughboy River, Australia, 64, 69
Dunedin, New Zealand, 12, 13, 17
Durack River, El Questro, 50, 53
Dylup Plantation, New Guinea, 88–90, 92, 94

Efaté, The Island of, 6, 78, 79
El Questro, 6, 45–53, 60
Emma Gorge, El Questro, 45, 47, 49, 50, 52
Eskdale, Australia, 21, 25

Fiji, 80, 82
Fin-Nor, Fishing Reels, 32, 40, 62, 70, 74
Flies,
    Dry,
        BlackGnat, 16
        Black Muddler, 16

        Elk-hair Caddis, 22, 25
        Kakahi Queen, 16, 22, 25
        Red Ant, 22, 25
        Royal Wuff, 9, 16, 17, 22, 25
    Nymphs,
        Black, 19
        Brown, 22, 25
        Hare and Copper, 6, 16
    Saltwater,
        Barra Clouser, 40, 41, 42
        Blue Deceiver, 84
        Chartreuse Deceiver, 84, 90, 93
        Cockroach Deceiver, 50–52
        Crazy Charlie, 55, 60, 62
        Darwin Deceiver, 49–51
        Goose Creek Deceiver, 27, 32, 33, 35, 55, 60, 61, 63, 67, 69–71, 93
        Green Deceiver, 49, 50
        Harro's Deceiver, 40, 41
        Pink Thing, 40–42, 49–53, 63, 67, 69
        Sauri Fly, 27, 32–34, 40, 41, 55, 60–62, 84, 93
        Thong Popper, 63, 67, 69
        Whitebait Deceiver, 27, 32, 33
        Yellow Deceiver, 27, 32, 33
Fly-fish (-erman/men, -ing), 8, 9, 16, 29, 32, 35, 38, 40, 45, 56, 57, 59, 62, 64, 68, 69, 72, 77, 80, 81, 84, 90

Gibb, Graeme, 6, 24, 25
Great Barrier Reef, Australia, 28, 32, 35
Great Dividing Range, Australia, 20
Guiding (Guides), 16, 21, 24, 38, 44, 49, 88

Haines,
    Don, 6, 17
    Gayle, 17
Hamilton, Jason, 6, 49, 52
Hankow Reef, New Guinea, 93
Hardy, Aree, 6
Hardy (Tackle), 40, 50
Hawea (River, Town), New Zealand, 17
Hawkdun Range, New Zealand, 9, 13
Helicopter (Heli-fishing), 45, 47–50, 53
Hermitage Motor Inn, Australia, 21, 24
Hole, Gini, 6, 52, 53
Hydroelectric (-ity, Schemes), 9, 14, 20

Ida Range, New Zealand, 9, 13
IGFA, 65, 93, 94
Indian Ocean, 56, 59
Insects,
    Caddis, 11, 17, 21
    Dun, 21
    Spinner, 21

Jackson River, Australia, 64, 68, 69

Kakanui Range, New Zealand, 9
Kakar Island, New Guinea, 89–93
Khancoban, Australia, 21, 24
Kiewa River, Australia, 20, 22, 25
Kimberley, The, Australia, 45, 48, 49, 52, 53, 89
King River, Australia, 21, 22, 24
King River, El Questro, 50
Knight, Signa, 6, 58, 60, 61
Knots,
    Australian Connection, 76
    Barrel-rolled Knot, 76
    Bimini Twist, 40, 49, 76
    Half-hitch, 76
    Loop-to-loop, 76
    Non-slip Knot, 76
    Surgeons Loop, 76
Kreh, Lefty, 32, 72, 73
Kulili Plantation, New Guinea, 89, 90, 92–94
Kununurra, Australia, 45, 48, 49, 52, 53

Lammerlaw Mountains, New Zealand, 9, 13
Lammermore Mountains, New Zealand, 9
Licences, 14, 16, 22, 25, 83
Lindis Pass, New Zealand, 17
Lizard Island, Australia, 6, 27–29, 31–35, 40
Lizard Island Research Station, 28, 29, 31, 32, 34, 35
Loomis (tackle), 32, 40, 70, 73

Mackerel, 29, 32, 34, 35, 38, 44, 65, 83
Madang, New Guinea, 87–90, 92, 94
Malaria, 84, 93
Mangrove Jack, 38, 40, 44, 64, 65
Maniototo, New Zealand, 9, 11–14, 17, 69
Manuherikia River, New Zealand, 13
Marlin, 8, 29, 34, 72, 73, 77, 80, 84, 85, 87, 90, 92
'Marlin Highway', The, Vanuatu, 81–86
McDonald River, Australia, 64
Melbourne, Australia, 20, 21, 31, 33, 37, 80, 82
Middleton,
    Anna, 6, 92, 94
    Brett, 6, 88, 90, 92–94
    Derrick, 89
    John, 6, 92
Mitchell, Stephen, 6, 41, 44
Mitta Mitta River, Australia, 19, 21, 22, 24, 25

Monaro, Australia, 20
Mount Beauty, Australia, 21, 22, 25
Mount Clear, Australia, 20
Mudcrabs, 65, 71

Naseby, New Zealand, 13
New Zealand, 9, 12, 17, 28, 31, 64, 65, 80
North Rough Ridge Range, New Zealand, 9
Northern Territory, Australia, 35, 36, 52

Omarama, New Zealand, 12, 13, 17
Onslow, Lake, New Zealand, 14
Otematata, New Zealand, 13
Ovens River, Australia, 22

Pakula, Peter, 6, 90, 92
Palmerston, New Zealand, 12, 17
Papua New Guinea (New Guinea), 6, 49, 75, 77, 85, 87–90, 92, 93
Patearoa, New Zealand, 11–13, 17
Pentecost River, El Questro, 47, 48, 50, 52
Percy, Bob, 6, 58, 60
Perth, Australia, 45, 49, 53, 56, 58, 60
Phillips, Mitchell, 6, 68–70
Pineapple Flat, Australia, 24
Poolburn Reservoir, New Zealand, 11, 14
Pontynen, Robyn, 6, 33
Porter,
    Vance, 6, 68–70
    Patrick, 6, 68–70
Port Essington, Australia, 36–38, 40, 41
Port Moresby, New Guinea, 87–90, 94

Qantas, 12, 29, 94
Queenfish, 38, 43, 44, 64, 65, 68, 69 83
Queensland, Australia, 28, 64, 65
Queenstown New Zealand, 12

Raggedy Range, New Zealand, 9, 13
Rainbow Runner, 93
Ranfurly (Hotel, Motel, Town), New Zealand, 12, 13, 17
Recipes, 17, 26, 35, 44, 53, 62, 70, 86, 93
Reddy, Mick, 6, 44
Redfin, 19
Ribbon Fish, 65, 68
Rock and Pillar Range, New Zealand, 9
Rose River, Australia, 21, 24, 25
Royal Flying Doctor Service, 29, 31, 53

Sailfish, 29, 72, 90
Scholz,
    Gary, 6, 24, 25
    Susan, 6
Seisia, Australia, 64, 68, 71
Seven Spirit (Bay, Lodge, Wilderness P/L), 6, 35, 36–44, 49, 50
Shag River, New Zealand, 17

Shark, 33, 61, 65, 71
Skardon River, Australia, 64, 69
Sooty Grunter, 49, 52, 53, 65
Spry,
    Mike, 21, 24
    Will, 16
Swain, Bret, 6, 40, 41, 43
Sydney, Australia, 6, 12, 20, 21, 28, 31, 33, 37, 53, 64, 67, 68, 80, 82, 88, 89, 90, 91, 94
System II Reels, 32, 40, 50, 70

Taieri River, New Zealand 13, 16
Talio, 6, 89, 91–93
Tarpon, 38, 49, 65
Teasers, 33, 34, 73, 75–77, 84, 85, 92, 93
Thomson,
    Brian, 6, 17
    Christine, 6, 17
Thomson,
    Marcus, 6, 81–86
    Vicki, 6, 81, 84, 86
Threadfin Salmon, 50
Todd, E. J., 6
Trepang Bay, New Zealand, 38, 41, 43, 44
Trevally, 29, 32, 38, 40, 41, 44, 59, 61, 64, 65, 69, 83
Trout,
    Brown, 9, 11, 16, 17, 21, 22, 25
    Coral, 61, 65
    Rainbow, 14, 19, 21, 22, 25
Tuku Tuku Ranch, Vanuatu, 80–82, 84, 85
Tuna,
    Dogtooth, 93, 94
    General, 29, 38, 40, 44, 57, 59, 64, 72, 90
    Northern Bluefin, 65, 70, 71
Twizel, New Zealand, 12, 13, 17

Vanuatu, 8, 77, 78, 80, 81, 83, 84, 86, 92, 94
Vashon Head, Australia, 38, 44
Victoria(n), Australia, 6, 19, 20, 21, 24, 25, 35, 49
Vila, Port, Vanuatu, 78, 80–84
Vrilya Point, Australia, 64, 68, 70

Wahoo, 57, 59, 61, 83
Waitaki (River, Valley), New Zealand, 12–14, 17
Waldron,
    Marg, 6
    Phil, 6
Wangaratta, Australia, 21, 24, 25
Weigall, Mark (The Trout School), 21, 24
Western Australia, 45, 48, 52, 57
West Island Lodge (Cocos Island), 57–62
Wolstenholme, Nick, 6, 24–26
Wyndham, Australia, 45, 49, 50

York Peninsula (Cape York), Australia, 64, 68